Stana

Stand

Putting on the full armour of God

Warren W. Wiersbe

10 Publishing
a division of 10 of those.com

First published in Great Britain in 2017

Previously published in 1986 by The Good News Broadcasting Association, Inc. under the title of What to Wear to the War

British Library Cataloguing in Publication Data
A record for this book is available from the British Library

ISBN: 978-1-911272-20-5

Designed and typeset by Pete Barnsley (Creative Hoot)

Printed and bound in Denmark by Nørhaven

10Publishing, a division of 10ofthose.com
Unit C, Tomlinson Road, Leyland, PR25 2DY, England

Email: info@10ofthose.com
Website: www.10ofthose.com

Contents

Chapter One:

Take a Stand!

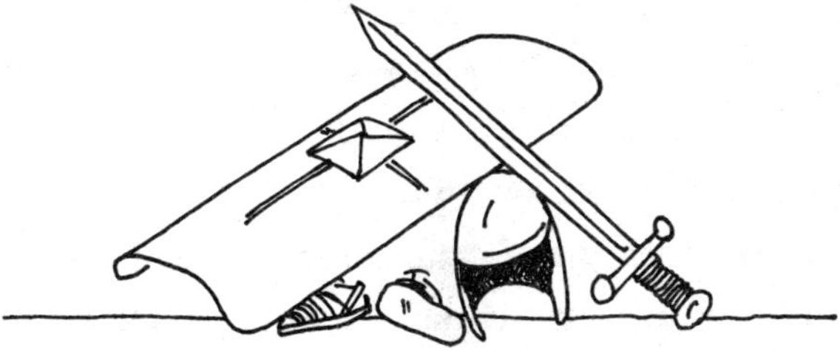

Finally, be strong in the Lord and in his mighty power. Put on the full armour of God so that you can take your stand against the devil's schemes.

(Eph. 6:10–11)

Some people reject the military side of the Christian life. I appreciate those who want to see peace on earth; however, as long as sin exists in this world, the battle between Satan's forces and

God's people will rage on. Anyone who chooses to be on the side of the Lord Jesus Christ will face severe opposition from Satan and his followers. And those who refuse to fight will fall in the heat of the battle.

The Bible frequently uses images of war to depict the Christian life. Paul exhorted Timothy to be a good soldier of Jesus Christ (see 2 Tim. 2:3). In fact, the first picture our Lord gave of the Church was a military one. He told the disciples that the gates of hell would not prevail against the onslaughts of the Church (see Matt. 16:18). In ancient times a common military tactic used by armies was to break down the gate of an enemy's fortress with a battering ram. Once inside, they could then destroy the opposing army. Likewise, Jesus told us that Satan and his forces are not able to withstand, or prevent, the onward march of Christianity. The Church *will* win the war.

The Soldier's Readiness

The Christian life is not a playground – it's a battleground and whether we like it or not, every Christian is called to be a soldier and to 'fight the good fight' (1 Tim. 6:12). No good soldier enters a battle without being fully prepared and protected. Likewise, God does not expect us to go to war unarmed. He has given us the armour and weapons we need for the fight, and He expects us to use them. Ephesians 6 tells us:

> *Finally, be strong in the Lord and in his mighty power. Put on the full armour of God, so that you can take your stand against the devil's schemes. For our struggle is not against flesh and blood, but against the rulers, against the authorities, against the powers of this dark world and against the spiritual forces of evil in the heavenly realms. Therefore put on the full armour of God, so that when the day of evil comes, you may be able to stand your ground, and after you have done everything, to stand (vv. 10–13).*

What is the armour of God that we are to wear? Paul went on to list the different parts of the armour that we are to put on by faith – the belt[a]

[a]This is 'girdle' in the original 1986 version of this book, but has been modernised to 'belt' throughout.

of truth, the breastplate of righteousness, the shoes of peace, the shield of faith, the helmet of salvation and the sword of the Spirit (see vv. 14–17).

While putting on this armour is important, our *posture* in battle is even more vital. Notice the emphasis Paul placed on the word 'stand' in this passage. We are told to 'stand firm' (v. 14), fully clothed in God's armour, so that we can take a 'stand against the devil's schemes' (v. 11) and 'so that when the day of evil comes, you may be able to stand your ground' (v. 13). Having done all this, we will then be able to stand (see v. 13).

Why this emphasis on standing? Many people misunderstand the purpose of the Christian's armour. The purpose of the armour is to help us stand so we don't lose the ground that Jesus has won for us. In fact, the entire book of Ephesians talks about our posture as Christians. The first three chapters describe the wealth that we have inherited through faith in Christ. Because of His grace, we have the privilege of being *seated* with Christ in the heavenly realms (see Eph. 2:6) and of sharing in His riches.

In chapter 4 Paul moves from talking about our wealth in Christ to our *walk* in Christ: 'I, therefore, the prisoner of the Lord, beseech you to walk worthy of the calling with which you were called' (v. 1, NKJV). Because today we have the privilege of sitting with Christ on His throne, we are able to walk in the will of God and according to the calling He has given us. This means that we are able to 'no longer walk as the rest of the Gentiles walk' (v. 17, NKJV) but instead should 'walk in love' (5:2, NKJV) 'as children of light' (v. 8, NKJV), being careful to 'walk circumspectly' (v. 15, NKJV).

Anyone who is seated with Christ on His throne and is walking with Him, revealing Him to an evil world, is going to be attacked by the Enemy. Spiritual *warfare* goes hand in hand with our wealth and our walk. The privilege of partaking in the riches of Christ's grace and glory as part of His Body is not without its responsibilities. We should not expect to *sit* and *walk* with Him unless we are also willing to *stand* for Him in the battle against Satan. He has already won the war for us – it's our responsibility to hold on to His victory.

It's important to remember that the purpose of our Christian armour is not for use in gaining new territory. Of course, we are involved in a conquest. When Jesus said, 'the gates of Hades will not overcome it' (Matt. 16:18), He was talking about the movement of His army, the Church, in gaining territory and claiming the spoil. But even as we are conquering, we must remember that we do not fight *for* victory but *from* victory. Christ has already won the victory for us, and we have already entered into our spiritual inheritance in Him. Thus, our role in the battle with the Devil is that of claiming and holding on to the territory and inheritance won for us by the Lord Jesus Christ.

We find a beautiful illustration of this truth in the book of Joshua. The Children of Israel were preparing to enter the Promised Land – their inheritance. God told Joshua, 'Now then, you and all these people, get ready to cross the Jordan River into the land I am about to give to them – to the Israelites. I will give you every place where you set your foot, as I promised Moses' (Josh. 1:2–3). In other words God was saying, 'Start walking. You already have the inheritance:

now claim it by faith.' While the Israelites had to fight the inhabitants of the land, they did not do it to conquer new territory but merely to claim the inheritance that God has already given them.

However, knowing the land was theirs and claiming it by faith was not enough. The Children of Israel also needed to have strength and courage. Three times in Joshua 1 we find the Lord telling Joshua to 'be strong and courageous' (vv. 6,9: see also v. 7). In telling the people about God's commands, Joshua gave them the same exhortation (see v. 18). Likewise, Paul gave us the same instructions for our spiritual warfare: 'Finally, be strong in the Lord and in his mighty power' (Eph. 6:10).

Having strength and courage is important not only for the battles but also for the so-called times of peace. It is at these times, when we have let down our defences, that Satan attacks the hardest and gains the most victories. This is what happened to the Israelites. Under Joshua's leadership, they conquered the land and claimed their inheritance. But a new generation came along that didn't appreciate their inheritance and didn't know the Lord as they should. Their strength and courage waned. As a result, they could not stand against their enemies, and they lost their inheritance.

Judges 2 tells us, 'After that whole generation had been gathered to their ancestors, another generation grew up who knew neither the LORD nor what he had done for Israel' (v. 10). Have you ever wondered how the people could forget the Lord and what He had done for them so quickly? It may be that the older generation had not kept the Lord's command to teach their children the Law given to them in the wilderness and to relate to them how He had brought them out of Egypt (see Deut. 6:6–25). Likewise, our responsibility as parents today is to teach the Word of God to our children so they might teach it to our grandchildren and our great-grandchildren.

It is also possible that the older generation taught the younger one but that the new generation didn't want to listen. They were content in the land and didn't think they needed God anymore. As a result, the Lord permitted them to be conquered by various nations – the inhabitants of Mesopotamia, the Moabites, the

Philistines, the Canaanites and the Midianites (see Judg. 3:8,12–13,31; 4:2; 6:1).

Time after time the Children of Israel would sin by rejecting God, and He would allow the surrounding nations to invade and take over their inheritance. Each time the Israelites were unable to stand against them: 'In his anger against Israel the LORD gave them into the hands of raiders who plundered them. He sold them into the hands of their enemies all around, whom they were no longer able to resist. Whenever Israel went out to fight, the hand of the LORD was against them to defeat them, just as he had sworn to them. They were in great distress' (2:14–15).

Why couldn't they take a stand against their enemies? Because they were bowing down to idols: 'Yet they would not listen to their judges but prostituted themselves to other gods and worshipped them' (v.17). Each time they were enslaved by other nations, they would cry out to God, and He would eventually send a judge to deliver them. But as soon as they had their land back, they would return to idol worship and other sins. They never learned their lesson and worshipped only the Lord.

Like the Israelites, we have a tremendous inheritance in Christ. How do we translate that wealth into a daily walk with Him? By bowing. When we bow down before the Lord in worship and pray to Him, then we are practising our position in Jesus Christ. Even though *positionally* we are seated with Him in the heavenly realms, *practically* we're still here on earth. The only way to translate that position into practise is by bowing before the Lord continually, remembering our inheritance in Him. When Paul considered everything Christ had done for him, he stated, 'For this reason I kneel before the Father' (3:14; see vv. 5–12). When we try to walk without first bowing before God, we will walk out of His paths and will lose ground. As a result, we will not be able to stand against the Enemy.

Before we can stand against Satan and his army, we must first bow before the Lord in prayer and worship and then put on the whole armour He has given us. We wear this armour, not to gain new territory but to prevent the Devil from robbing us of our inheritance. Satan wants to spoil and pillage our wealth and enslave us. But when we stand in the strength and power of the Lord, we will be victorious in our fight.

The Soldier's Responsibilities

As soldiers of Christ, we not only need to be ready for our ongoing battle with Satan, but we also have several responsibilities that we must fulfil if we are going to hold on to our inheritance and *fight from victory* – not *for* victory. Our responsibilities are threefold: (1) We must know our enemies; (2) we must use the equipment; and (3) we must depend on the energy that God provides.

Who is the Enemy? Ephesians 6:11 tells us, 'Put on the full armour of God, so that you can take your stand against the devil's schemes.' Paul then goes on to describe the Enemy we are fighting: 'For we wrestle not against flesh and blood, but against principalities, against powers, against the rulers of the darkness of this world, against spiritual wickedness in high places.' (v. 12, KJV). Satan is not merely a flesh and blood human or a concept of evil; he is a living, personal, literal being with the power to control people and to perform many evil deeds.

It is important to note that the phrase 'in high places' in verse 12 may also be translated 'in the heavenlies'. As we have already noted, because of Christ's grace, those who accept Him are seated with Him in the heavenly realms. God has blessed us with every spiritual resource and blessings because of our position in Christ. Yet here we learn that Satan also has access to the same heavenly realms. How? By his wiles, devices, strategies and craftiness. He attacks believers, trying to get us to doubt God's Word and to divide our allegiance to Him. Satan knows that if he can cause us to become fearful, then he can rob us of all the riches we have inherited. Knowing that we are seated on Christ's throne is worthless if we are afraid of the Enemy. Our fear enables the Devil to rob us of the enjoyment of our blessed position in Jesus Christ.

We have three spiritual enemies – the world, the flesh and the Devil. Paul made it clear in Ephesians 6:12 that our problem is not people: 'For our struggle is not against flesh and blood'. When strife and problems exist, our trouble is not with the person but with Satan, who is working in and through that person. Satan can even use a believer. He used Peter. When the apostle was trying to divert Jesus from His plan for mankind, Jesus said to Peter, 'Get behind me, Satan' (Matt. 16:23). The Devil used Ananias and Sapphira, filling them with greed and lies (see Acts 5:1–11). The Enemy loves to control us, causing us to do and say things we shouldn't.

Satan is not an abstraction. He is a real person, and he used people, including people in the Church. Ephesians 6 was not written to idol worshippers and unbelievers; it was written to people in the church at Ephesus. Satan wants to work in the Church, using it for his evil purposes. He is strong and powerful. In the Bible he is described as a lion, and dragon and a destroyer (see 1 Pet. 5:8; Rev. 20:2; 1 Cor. 10:10; Ps. 17:4; Jer. 4:7). His strategies and wiles are subtle and deadly. He is well organised; he has a whole army of demonic forces at his command. Therefore, we must know our Enemy, use the armour we have been given and depend on the energy and strength that God alone can provide if we are to win our war with Satan.

Chapter Two:

Do You Know Your Enemy?

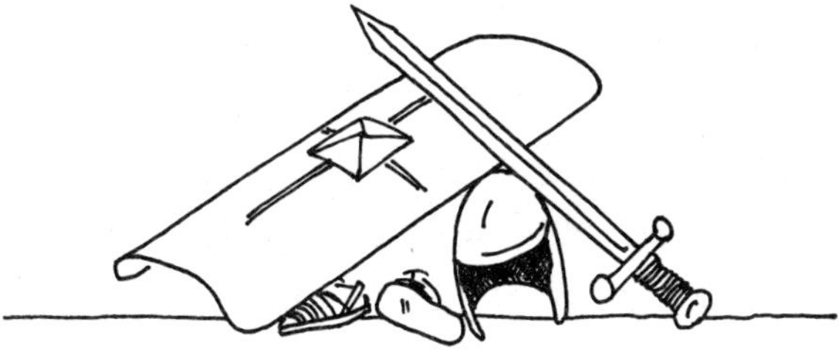

For our struggle is not against flesh and blood, but against the rulers, against the authorities, against the powers of this dark world and against the spiritual forces of evil in the heavenly realms. Therefore put on the full armour of God, so that when the day of evil comes, you may be able to stand your ground, and after you have done everything, to stand.

(Eph. 6:12–13)

Life is a battleground. The sooner you accept this truth, the easier it's going to be to win the battle. Satan is trying to destroy us because we are seated with Christ in the heavenly realms. We have all the riches and resources of the resurrected Christ available to us. We are like the people of Israel when they moved into the Promised Land and claimed their victory. When the older generation died, the new generation forgot about God and lost their territory. Why? They did not stand.

Grow Up

The Christian life is a growth process. Before we can walk with Christ and run the race set before us (see Heb. 12:1), we must first learn how to stand. Ephesians 6:11 (NKJV) tells us, 'Put on the whole armour of God, that you may be able to stand against the wiles of the devil.' The word 'wiles' can also be translated as 'methods' or 'craftiness'. The same word is used in Ephesians 4:14: 'Then we will no longer be infants, tossed back and forth by the waves, and blown here and there by every wind of teaching and by the cunning and craftiness of people in their deceitful scheming.'

In Ephesians 4:14, Paul stressed the importance of growing up and maturing as Christians. Those who don't mature are like small children. Children are very naïve. They believe anything or anyone. They lack the experience and education to exercise discernment. Unfortunately, some of God's children have no discernment either. They will listen to a television or radio evangelist or read a book by some author and will not have the discernment to recognise false doctrine. However, when we mature as believers, we will not be tricked and led astray by Satan's cunning craftiness and methodology.

Wear All of the Armour

How are we able to stand against Satan's strategies? By putting on the whole armour of God. 'Therefore put on the full armour of God' (Eph. 6:13). It is vital that we wear *all* of the armour God has given us and not just some of it. If we don't use all of the equipment, then Satan will attack us at some unguarded place.

The story is told of a soldier who learned this lesson the hard way. In 1586 a British soldier, Sir Philip Sidney, was fighting in the Netherlands.

He saw one of his friends fighting in the battle without his leg armour on, so he took his off. He was hit in the leg and died as a result. The enemy was able to find one small spot that was left unprotected, and attacked that area.

Often Christians fall into the trap of thinking that they don't need a certain piece of armour. However, if we leave any piece out, we are exercising pride. We are saying, 'Well, God, I don't need that part of the armour. I've got that area of my life under control.'

Have you ever noticed that when the great men and women of the Bible sinned, they always fell in the areas of their greatest strength? Abraham's greatest strength was his faith. That is where he failed. He lied about his wife (see Gen. 12:10–20). What was Moses' greatest strength? He was the meekest man on the earth. Yet he lost his temper, smote the rock instead of speaking to it and took the credit for producing the water. As a result, he lost the privilege of entering the Promised Land (see Num. 20:7–12). Likewise, Peter failed in his greatest area of strength – his courage. His faith and courage faltered when he was walking on the water (see

Matt. 14:25–31), but probably his greatest failure was his denial of the Lord Jesus Christ three times (see 26:69–75). What was David's greatest strength? His integrity. He was a man after God's own heart. That's where he failed. He moved into duplicity – lying and leading a double life (see 2 Sam. 11). When you begin to believe that you've conquered a certain area of your life and do not need God's protection for it, that's the very area where Satan will attack you.

We wrestle not against flesh and blood (see Eph. 6:12). We must remember that our conflict is not with people but with Satan, who uses people. While some people deny the existence of demonic powers, those of us who believe the Word of God know that these demonic powers exist. While Satan is not omniscient or omnipresent – he doesn't know everything and cannot be everywhere at the same time – he has such a huge army of demonic forces at his control that he can operate in many places at one time. With the help of these demonic powers, the Devil can accomplish his will.

We are wrestling against an organised demonic conspiracy – principalities, powers, rulers of the darkness of this world and spiritual wickedness in high places (see v. 12). Satan has access to the throne of God (see Job 1:6–2:8; Rev. 12). He wants to rob us of the inheritance we have in Christ. In order to successfully defend ourselves from his vicious attacks, we must learn to stand in the power of Christ and must put on all of God's armour. If we are not completely prepared and protected, he will destroy us.

Recognise Satan's Tactics

Whenever the Devil finds a Christian who is appropriating his wealth and practising his walk, he will attack that believer. How does he do it? We learn much about Satan's tactics by examining the different pieces of the Christian's armour. God has designed each part of the armour to protect us from the Enemy's many methods of warfare. Recognising Satan's tactics and using the appropriate pieces of armour will enable us to successfully defend ourselves in battle.

The first tactic that Satan successfully uses against us is *division*. He knows that if he can divide our loyalties so that we are not concentrating on the battle, then he can defeat us. Satan's greatest weapon is duplicity. That's why Jesus warned us so strongly against leading a double life. He stated, 'No one can serve two masters. Either you will hate the one and love the other, or you will be devoted to the one and despise the other. You cannot serve both God and Money' (Matt. 6:24). We cannot be looking in two directions at the same time – at God and at the world. Likewise, we cannot have our hearts and minds in heaven and on earth at the same time, for 'Such a person is double-minded and unstable in all they do' (Jas. 1:8).

What is our weapon against Satan's divisiveness? It is the belt of truth (see Eph. 6:14). The belt of truth speaks of integrity – of a soldier who is completely devoted to winning the battle. 'The finest armour is wasted on the soldier who has no will to fight', Geoffrey Wilson once stated. If we do not have the integrity to see the battle to its completion, then the rest of our armour will do us no good. Our whole life must be pulled together by truth.

Satan is not only the divider, but he is also the *denouncer* and *accuser*. He loves to stand before the throne of God and accuse His children.

He also works in our consciences, constantly reminding us of our past mistakes and sins. We need the breastplate of righteousness to ward off these accusations (see v. 14). If we do not remember that we have been justified and made righteous in Christ, we will not have an answer to Satan's accusations. We will begin to dwell on our past mistakes instead of living for Christ today, and Satan will have defeated us.

When Satan attempts to divide our loyalties, we have the belt of truth to protect us. In addition, the breastplate of righteousness enables us to defend ourselves against his accusations. The third piece of armour is the shoes of peace: 'having shod your feet with the preparation of the gospel of peace' (v.15, NKJV). If we are going to stand, we must have the right shoes. Interestingly enough, these are shoes of *peace*. Can you imagine a soldier wearing shoes of peace? However, Satan is the *destroyer*. He wants to move in and bring war. As Christian soldiers, we are not armoured for battle against good or good people. We are armoured for battle against Satan and evil and the only way to combat evil is by doing good. Likewise, the only antidote for war is peace. Because we are standing in peace and resting in the finished work of the Lord Jesus Christ, Satan cannot destroy us.

Not only does Satan try to divide, denounce and destroy us, but he also uses *doubt* as a means of defeating us. He loves to throw the fiery darts of doubt at us. I must confess that Satan uses this tactic against me frequently. Often when I've been seated on the platform in a church service or at a Bible conference, I have had a flaming arrow of doubt shoot into my thoughts.

What can we do when we are being attacked by doubts? We need to use the shield of faith to ward off these darts: 'In addition to all this, take up the shield of faith, with which you can extinguish all the flaming arrows of the evil one' (v. 16). Martin Luther used to say, 'I cannot stop the birds from flying around my head, but I can stop them from making a nest in my hair.' While we can't stop these fiery darts of doubt from being thrown at us, we can protect ourselves with the shield of faith. Faith in what? Faith in the Word of God and in the God of the Word. The Lord said to Abraham, 'Do not be afraid, Abram. I am your shield' (Gen. 15:1). When we have faith in the power of God, He will shield us from Satan's attacks and give us victory.

Besides throwing doubts at us, Satan likes to discourage us. He is the greatest *discourager*. He assails us with setbacks and frustrations until we are ready to quit. Satan knows that when a soldier loses hope, he has lost the battle.

What can we do to fight this feeling of discouragement and hopelessness? We need to take the helmet of salvation (see Eph. 6:17). The word 'salvation' means 'victory'. God is handing us His helmet of salvation. All we need to do is receive it. In 1 Thessalonians 5:8, this is called the hope of salvation. When we have experienced God's salvation, we have hope to keep us going in the midst of discouragement. We know that our Conqueror is coming and that one day He will deliver us. Thus, the saints of God cannot be discouraged as long as they are thinking about the blessed hope of Jesus Christ's return.

Denial is another of Satan's tactics that he successfully uses against the Christian. He denies the faith. He denies the resurrection. He denies everything the Word of God teaches us. How can we combat Satan's denials? By using the sword of the Spirit – the Word of God (see Eph. 6:17). When Jesus was tempted by the Devil in the wilderness, He used this sword. In each of the three temptations, Jesus responded with the words, 'It is written' (see Matt. 4:4,7,10). He quoted passages from the book of Deuteronomy, and Satan was defenceless against this weapon. The Bible tells us that 'The word of God is alive and active. Sharper than any double-edged sword' (Heb. 4:12). When Satan tries to cause us to deny our faith, we need to take the sword of the Spirit and answer his denials with God's affirmations – 'It is written'.

Depend on God's Energy

Satan is using every evil tactic he can think of to defeat us. This is why we need the whole armour of God. But it is not enough just to know the Enemy and to use the equipment the Lord has given us. We must also depend on the energy that God provides. Ephesians 6:18 tells us, 'And pray in the Spirit on all occasions with all kinds of prayers and requests. With this in mind, be alert and always keep on praying for all the Lord's people.'

Why should we pray for *all* of the Lord's people? Because we are all in the same battle. Are you praying for all of the Lord's people? Or do you just pray for those in your family, in your church or in your denomination? Do we dare pray for the Lord's people in other groups? I think we should. In fact, we are commanded to. Why? They are fighting the same battle we are, and if they fall, it affects us. Thus, as God's people, we must never rejoice when a fellow soldier falls. Because if a fellow soldier falls, the Devil has just gained one more foothold.

We gain renewed energy and strength for the battle through prayer. That's why we are told to 'pray continually' (1 Thess. 5:17). When we pray, we should not only make requests of God, but also we should spend time in thanksgiving and praise to Him and in making supplications for others.

It is also vital that we are attentive at all times, including our times of prayer. Jesus warned us, 'Watch and pray so that you will not fall into temptation' (Matt. 26:41). The Devil is prowling about like a roaring lion, waiting to devour us (see 1 Pet. 5:8). We need to pray with all perseverance. We must always pray and not faint (see Luke 18:1).

Prayer is the means by which we receive God's unlimited source of energy. Why do we need this energy? Because we are living in the evil day: 'Therefore put on the full armour of God, so that when the day of evil comes, you may be able to stand your ground, and after you have done everything, to stand' (Eph. 6:13). Why is the day evil? Because Satan is the god of this age. God is still on the throne, but He is permitting Satan to do his work. However, in the end, God is going to be the victor.

Why must we be strong in the Lord? Because the Enemy is strong, because the day is evil, because the outcome is serious. We are fighting a battle. However, too many people today are trying to live on substitutes rather than depending on God's strength and resources. We must be strong because the outcome is serious for God. Is He going to receive the glory? The outcome is serious for us. Are we going to be victors or victims? And the outcome is serious for others. Are we going to be stumbling blocks or stepping stones for them? Why must we be strong? Because Jesus paid dearly for our victory. Put on the armour He has bought for you, and claim the victory in Him.

Chapter Three:

Satan Hates Integrity

The Belt of Truth

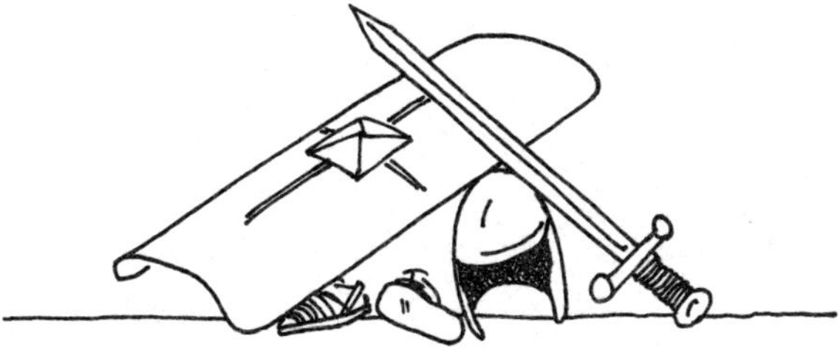

Stand firm then, with the belt of truth buckled around your waist, with the breastplate of righteousness in place

(Eph. 6:14)

Christians are waging a fierce war with Satan. Our Enemy is strong, and his tactics are deceptive. In order to claim the victory that Christ won for us at Calvary, we must stand up and put on the spiritual armour God has given us for the battle.

Let's examine this armour and see how we can use it to ward off Satan's attacks. The first piece of the Christian soldier's armour is the belt of truth: 'Stand firm then, with the belt of truth buckled round your waist' (Eph. 6:14).

The belt that Paul was speaking of here was worn by Roman soldiers. It was not simply a strip of cloth around his waist or even a narrow belt. Instead, it was generally a leather apron that helped to protect the lower part of his body. The belt was also used as a sheath for the soldier's sword.

What does the belt of truth illustrate in the life of the believer? In the Bible, a belt had the function of pulling things together. In the culture of that day, both men and women, including soldiers, wore flowing robes. When they wanted to move rapidly, the people would gather up their robes and tuck the ends into their belts so their legs would be unencumbered. Likewise, the Christian must prepare his mind and heart for battle, eliminating any thoughts or habits that would hinder his walk with the Lord. Peter has this idea in mind when he wrote: 'Therefore gird up the loins of your mind, be sober, and rest your hope fully upon the grace that is to be brought to you at the revelation of Jesus Christ' (1 Pet. 1:13, NKJV).

The belt of truth represents a life and mind that is pulled together and ready to serve for the glory of God. It speaks of integrity – truth in the inner being. David described this kind of integrity in Psalm 51:6 when he said, 'Yet you desired faithfulness even in the womb'. It's not enough just to carry the sword of the Spirit – the Word of God. The truth of God's Word must penetrate our lives so that our actions and motives are governed by integrity and truth.

Paul had much to say about this truth in his letters. In Ephesians 4:14–15 he told the believers that instead of being tossed about by every wind of doctrine they should speak the truth in love in order to become like Christ. Later he added that the truth is in Christ Jesus (see v. 21). The truth that the apostle was speaking of in these passages is integrity – that settled conviction of life that leads us in the right direction.

The opposite of integrity is duplicity. Duplicity is hypocrisy – trying to lead a double life. We try to focus our minds and hearts on God and on worldly pleasures at the same time. But this kind of double vision always leads to unfaithfulness. We cannot serve two masters (see Matt. 6:24). Only the soldier who has directed all his energies towards one goal – winning the battle – will be victorious. Paul had this singleness of purpose in his life. He stated, 'But one thing I do: forgetting what is behind and straining towards what is ahead, I press on towards the goal to win the prize for which God has called me heavenwards in Christ Jesus' (Phil. 3:13–14).

Of course, Jesus Christ is our best example of a life of integrity. In describing the coming Messiah, the Prophet Isaiah wrote: 'Righteousness will be his belt and faithfulness the sash round his waist' (Isa. 11:5). Throughout His life on earth, Jesus had only one purpose and goal in mind: '"My food," said Jesus, "is to do the will of him who sent me and to finish his work"' (John 4:34).

If we are going to stand our ground against Satan and his forces, we must declare our allegiance to Christ and maintain our integrity.

The minute we display any division or duplicity in our lives, we have given Satan an opening where he can attack us. Once he gains a foothold, his influence in our lives gradually grows until he finally controls us.

Let's examine the belt of truth (integrity) and learn how we can apply it to our lives. In looking at this piece of the Christian's armour, we will also meet three winners and three losers in the battle of life. These winners in the Bible won because they put on the belt of integrity, while the losers lost because they practised duplicity.

The Danger of Doubles

What is integrity? I think one of the best illustrations of the difference between integrity and duplicity can be found in mathematics. In mathematics, a whole number is called an integer, while part of a number is called a fraction. Thus, integrity means a whole person – one who is complete and undivided.

In Matthew 6:19–21, Jesus spoke to us about this matter of duplicity and integrity. He stated, 'Do not store up for yourselves treasures on earth … . But store up for yourselves treasures in heaven … . For where your treasure is, there your heart will be also.' Jesus made it clear in this passage that we cannot have a divided heart. We can't look for the pleasures of this world and for the joys of the Christian life at the same time. We can store treasures in only one place. God has given us all things richly to enjoy (see 2 Tim. 6:17), and He does want us to enjoy life; however, He doesn't want us to focus our hearts and energies on gaining all these temporary pleasures. Our heart can be in only one place, and that place should be with the Lord.

In addition to the danger of having a double heart, Jesus also warned us about having a double mind. He said, 'The eye is the lamp of the body. If your eyes are healthy, your whole body will be full of light. But if your eyes are unhealthy, your whole body will be full of darkness. If then the light within you is darkness, how great is that darkness!' (Matt. 6:22–23). In this passage Jesus was describing a person with double vision – someone who tries to look in two directions at the same time. Of course, when he attempts to do this, he can see nothing clearly. Spiritually, the eye represents our outlook. If our outlook is not healthy, then we are not going to be healthy inwardly. Our outlook determines our outcome. Those whose minds and outlooks are divided will be unstable in everything they do (see Jas. 1:8).

Not only should believers beware of having a double heart and a double mind, but we must also guard against having a double will. We cannot have divided loyalties. Jesus stated, 'No one can serve two masters. Either you will hate the one and love the other, or you will be devoted to the one and despise the other. You cannot serve both God and Money' (Matt. 6:24).

What causes worry in people's lives? Duplicity. They have double hearts. They love the treasures of this world while trying to love the Lord. They are double minded. They have one eye on heaven and one eye on the earth. They want to have the best of both worlds. They are double willed. One minute they're serving God, and the next minute they're serving their own interests. However, this kind of living does not work; it pulls your life apart.

The only solution for the problem of duplicity is integrity. How can we have integrity?

By practising the greatest of all commandments: 'Love the Lord your God with all your heart and with all your soul and with all your mind and with all your strength' (Mark 12:30). This is integrity. It means putting on the belt of truth and saying, 'I am totally devoted to the Lord. I don't have another master. I am looking only to Jesus, the Author and Finisher of my faith. I love Him with all of my heart; I listen to Him with all of my attention; I understand His Word with all of my mind; and I want to do His will with all of my will.' It is so easy for us to have a dual allegiance. Instead of building our house on the rock, we build part of the house on the rock and part of the house on the sand, and then we wonder why things fall apart.

Winners and Losers

In understanding how integrity can help us defeat Satan, it will be helpful to look at some people in the Bible who were victorious because they put on the belt of truth. We will also look at others who were defeated because they did not have it on. We will see from their example why the belt of truth is so important on the battlefield.

The first war in the Bible is found in Genesis 14. Abraham became involved in that war because Lot, his nephew, had been captured by the opposing army. Abraham won the war and delivered Lot, but why was Lot captured in the first place? Why was he found in the wrong camp? Because he was double minded.

We find Lot's background in Genesis 13. He was afflicted with double vision – he had one eye on the heavenly city and one eye on Sodom. Genesis 13:10 says, 'Lot looked around and saw that the whole plain of the Jordan towards Zoar was well watered, like the garden of the LORD, like the land of Egypt. (This was before the LORD destroyed Sodom and Gomorrah.)'

Lot had taken off the belt of truth and had lost his integrity. Why? Because he had a double minded approach to life. He had his eyes on the land and how rich he could become instead of having his eyes on the Lord. He drifted off into wicked Sodom. When the people of Sodom were taken captive, Lot could do nothing about it. He didn't have any armour to protect him. As a result, He lost ground. He was forced to depend on Abraham, a man with integrity, to deliver him.

We can see Abraham's integrity when the king of Sodom came out to meet him. The king said to Abraham, 'Take all the wealth (the spoils of battle) that you want' (see 14:21).

However, Abraham replied, 'I made up my mind before this battle ever started that I wouldn't take so much as a shoelace from you' (see vv. 22–23). That's integrity! Abraham didn't go out to battle thinking, *I wonder what I'm going to get out of this.* His only thoughts were about rescuing his nephew, Lot. Abraham was a winner, while Lot was a loser.

Another illustration is found in Joshua 5. Before the battle of Jericho, Joshua was out assessing the situation. 'Now when Joshua was near Jericho, he looked up and saw a man standing in front of him with a drawn sword in his hand. Joshua went up to him and asked, "Are you for us or for our enemies?"' (v. 13). Joshua had integrity. He didn't think, *I wonder whose side he's on and whether or not I can pacify him. I wonder if I can do a little politicking here.* No, he pointedly asked, 'Whose side are you on?' Like Joshua, when you go out to fight the battle and face the Enemy, you'd better have on the belt of truth and know which side you're on.

Throughout his life, Joshua's integrity and loyalty to God never wavered. Just before his death, he urged the people, 'Now fear the LORD and serve him with all faithfulness' (24:14). No wonder Joshua was able to defeat his enemies and conquer the land.

Joshua's life stands in stark contrast to that of Achan, a soldier in Joshua's army (see ch. 7). Achan was double minded. He didn't enter the battle because he wanted to win a victory for the Lord; he was wondering what he could get for himself. He had a double heart. Part of his heart loved wealth and material possessions more than God. The Lord had instructed the Israelites to take no spoils from the battle but to dedicate everything to Him (see 6:18–19). However, when Achan saw the great wealth of Jericho, he stole some of it and buried it under his tent (see 7:20–21). He was double willed. He was trying to serve two masters. What happened? It killed him. He was responsible for the defeat of the whole army when they went to fight Ai. When Joshua discovered that their defeat was due to sin in the camp, Achan's sin was uncovered, and he and his family were stoned and burned along with all they owned (see vv. 24–26).

A third example of the results of integrity and of duplicity can be seen in the lives of David and Saul. Have you ever wondered why God chose David to replace Saul as king? Psalm 78:70–72 gives us the answer: 'He chose David his servant and took him from the sheepfolds; from tending the sheep he brought him to be the shepherd of his people Jacob, of Israel his inheritance. And David shepherded them with integrity of heart; with skilful hands he led them.' David had integrity. David's life teaches us that it doesn't matter how skilful our hands may be. If we don't have integrity in our hearts, God can't use us.

David went from victory to victory because he was a man of integrity. As David prepared to face Goliath, Saul wanted him to wear his armour. But David replied, 'I cannot go in these … because I am not used to them' (see 1 Sam. 17:38–39). Rather than trusting in human protection and resources, David put on the belt of truth and was able to defeat the enemy in battle after battle. Why was David victorious?

Because he had integrity and trusted in God rather than in his own abilities. He was a man after God's own heart (see Acts 13:22).

David's life was vastly different from that of Saul, the first king of Israel. Saul didn't have integrity. While David sought the will of God, Saul was always devising some scheme or plot. David stood firm, but Saul continually vacillated. When David sinned, he humbly confessed it to God. However, Saul only made excuses for his sins. Because Saul tried to live a double life, God rejected him as king. The Lord could not bless Saul because he refused to put on the belt of truth.

Satan loves duplicity, for he knows that a 'household divided against itself will not stand' (Matt. 12:25). We must decide, once and for all, that we are going to be completely yielded to Jesus Christ. Paul wrote concerning the life of a Christian soldier: 'Join with me in suffering, like a good soldier of Christ Jesus. No one serving as a soldier gets entangled in civilian affairs, but rather tries to please his commanding officer' (2 Tim. 2:3–4). A good soldier of Christ concentrates only on following the orders of his Commander. When we have this integrity, this singleness of purpose, Satan's weapons are useless against us.

There are no exceptions or compromises to God's explicit standards of morality. No matter what others may say or do, we need to stand firmly on God's side, saying, 'But as for me and my household, we will serve the LORD' (Josh. 24:15). When we put on this belt of truth and stand firm in our integrity, we can enter the battle boldly, knowing that Satan is powerless against us.

Chapter Four:

Silence the Accuser

The Breastplate of Righteousness

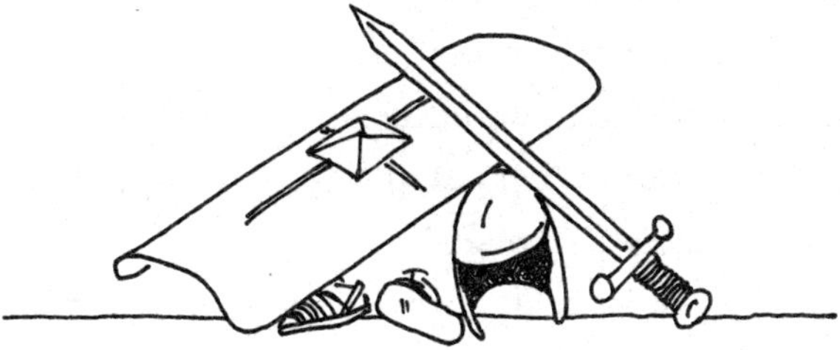

Stand firm then, with the belt of truth buckled around your waist, with the breastplate of righteousness in place

(Eph. 6:14)

Satan is a liar and accuser. He loves to destroy our Christian witness to the world with his accusations. He torments our minds, reminding us of our past mistakes and sins. When we begin to dwell on these past sins, then we forget the forgiveness we have received and feel that we are not worthy to serve the Lord. And once again, Satan has defeated us.

However, God has given us the weapon we need to silence our accuser – the breastplate of righteousness. Ephesians 6:13–14 admonishes the believer, 'Therefore put on the full armour of God, so that when the day of evil comes, you may be able to stand your ground, and after you have done everything, to stand. Stand firm then, with the belt of truth buckled round your waist, with the breastplate of righteousness in place'.

The breastplate was very important to a Roman soldier. It was a coat of mail that covered the front and back of a soldier's body from the neck to the thighs. Some have taught that the Christian doesn't have any armour to protect the back and, therefore, he should not turn around and run. But Paul was thinking of a Roman soldier when he wrote the letter to the Ephesians. The breastplate he was writing about covered the entire upper body and protected all the vital organs from injury.

The Christian soldier's coat of mail is the righteousness of God received by faith in Jesus Christ. This is what is known as imputed righteousness. In the Bible we find two kinds of righteousness – *imputed and imparted.* Imputed righteousness is part of *justification* – that which God gives us by faith. Imparted righteousness is *sanctification* – that which we live out in our daily lives. When righteousness is imputed to us the life of Christ within us imparts the desire to pursue righteousness.

Romans 3:19–24 gives us a description of God's imputed righteousness:

> *Now we know that whatever the law says, it says to those who are under the law, so that every mouth may be silenced and the whole world held accountable to God. Therefore no one will be declared righteous in God's sight by the works of the law; rather, through the law we become conscious of our sin. But now apart from the law the righteousness of God has been made known, to which the Law*

> *and the Prophets testify. This righteousness is given through faith in Jesus Christ to all who believe. There is no difference between Jew and Gentile, for all have sinned and fall short of the glory of God, and all are justified freely by his grace through the redemption that came by Christ Jesus.*

Imputed righteousness means God puts His righteousness on your account. He not only goes to the record book and erases your old record completely, but He also makes sure that nothing else is written on that page by filling it with His righteousness. Once the entry has been made, the matter is settled once and for all. Thus, when you turn to your page in the book and find your name written there, you will also find underneath it the words, 'Righteous in Jesus Christ.' This is imputed righteousness.

Once you have been declared righteous, you should demonstrate that righteousness in your daily life. Paul wrote about the importance of having imparted righteousness in Romans 6:12–14.

Therefore do not let sin reign in your mortal body so that you obey its evil desires. Do not offer any part of yourself to sin as an instrument of wickedness, but rather offer yourselves to God as those who have been brought from death to life; and offer every part of yourself to him as an instrument of righteousness. For sin shall no longer be your master, because you are not under the law, but under grace.

In this passage Paul was speaking of the need to have practical, everyday righteousness in our words, our walk, our motives, and in all we say and do. But while we need to live righteously because of the righteousness we have received from God, we must remember that our own righteousness is never good enough by itself.

Paul had learned this lesson well. He told the Philippians, 'If someone else thinks they have reasons to put confidence in the flesh, I have more' (Phil. 3:4). He then went on to give his pedigree and credentials. He was a circumcised Jew, a 'Hebrew of Hebrews' (v. 5). He had been a devout Pharisee who had zealously followed and upheld the Law, even to the point of persecuting the Church (see vv. 5–6). He had believed that he was righteous: 'as for righteousness based on the law, faultless' (v. 6). But then he met the Lord Jesus

Christ, and he considered all this to be rubbish so he might come to know Jesus personally (see vv. 7–8). In comparison to Christ, Paul realised that his righteousness was worthless in and of itself. He was willing to sacrifice it all in order that he might 'be found in him, not having a righteousness of my own that comes from the law, but that which is through faith in Christ – the righteousness that comes from God on the basis of faith' (v. 9).

Satan Accuses Us

Each day we need to put on the breastplate of righteousness by faith and reaffirm our position in Jesus Christ. We must depend on the righteousness of Christ rather than on our own good deeds. Why do we need this righteousness? Because Satan is the accuser. He is continually denouncing God's people. We desperately need this breastplate because apart from the righteousness of God through faith in Jesus Christ we cannot stand against the Evil One.

In Bunyan's *Pilgrim's Progress*, we find an important lesson about righteousness. The main character, Christian, is on his way to the

Holy City. Along the way he meets Apollyon (Satan). Satan tells him, 'Thou hast already been unfaithful in thy service to him (God); and how dost thou think to receive wages of him?'

Christian replies, 'Wherein, O Apollyon, have I been unfaithful to him?'

And Satan answers, 'Thou didst faint at first setting out, when thou wast almost choked in the Gulf of Despond; thou didst attempt wrong ways to be rid of thy burden, whereas thou shouldst have stayed till thy Prince had taken it off; thou didst sinfully sleep and lose thy choice thing; thou wast also almost persuaded to go back at the sight of the lions; and when thou talkest of thy journey, and of what thou hast heard and seen, thou art inwardly desirous of vain-glory in all that thou sayest or doest.'

Here Apollyon was reminding Christian of his many sins. He accused him of being unfaithful. But notice Christian's response: 'All this is true; and much more which thou hast left out: but the Prince whom I serve and honour is merciful and ready to forgive. But besides, these infirmities possessed me in thy country, . . . and I have groaned under them, been sorry for them, and have obtained pardon of my Prince.' Christian was claiming the breastplate of righteousness. Because he had this protection, Satan's accusations did not shake his faith.

Revelation 12:10 tells us, 'Then I heard a loud voice in heaven say: "Now have come the salvation and the power and the kingdom of our God, and the authority of his Messiah. For the accuser of our brothers and sisters, who accuses them before our God day and night, has been hurled down."' Satan is the accuser. He accuses us before God, and he accuses God before us. When he talks to God about us, he tells the truth, because he knows the truth. However, when he talks to us about God, he lies. He twists circumstances and biblical truths, making us blame God for things He didn't say or do.

We Accuse Ourselves

Satan is the accuser. However, unlike the characters in Bunyan's book, Satan does not accuse us face to face. His strategies are much more deceptive. I believe that Satan accuses us in three ways. First, he denounces us by encouraging us to accuse ourselves.

Some Christians have a problem with perpetual introspection. This constant self-examination is dangerous because it often leads to self-accusation. The Devil knows that if he can get you to accuse yourself – to dwell on the memories of past sins – then he has won the battle.

One day after I had completed a radio programme, I received a phone call from a woman who said, 'I sinned grievously when I was a young lady, and I really don't know what I should do. I've been asked to teach a Sunday school class, and I don't think I'm worthy to teach it. What do you think I should do?'

I asked her, 'Are you a Christian?'

'Oh, yes,' she replied, 'I have trusted the Lord.'

'What did the Lord do about those sins you committed as a young lady?'

'Well, I guess they are forgiven and gone.'

'Then serve the Lord,' I urged her.

This woman was allowing Satan to use her memories to accuse her. If you don't put on the breastplate of righteousness every day, your memory is going to accuse you day and night. If you dwell on these memories, you will end up putting yourself on a shelf, and God won't be able to use you. You will lose ground to the Devil.

Besides our memories of past mistakes, Satan also uses our feelings to accuse us. When we are run down from lack of sleep, poor eating habits, lack of exercise or illness, we have a tendency to give in to feelings of depression, self-pity or anger. It's at these times, when we are feeling depressed, that the Devil comes to us and says, 'That's right! Keep throwing fuel on the fire. You have a right to feel sorry for yourself. Remember all the things you've done and all the things people have done to you.' Before you know it, you are defeated.

What is the answer when we begin to accuse ourselves? The breastplate of righteousness. God knows our struggles better than we do or Satan does. We can take these memories and feelings to Him. What does the Lord do about them? He puts them under the blood of Jesus Christ. They are gone. He buries them in the depths of the sea (see Mic. 7:19). He blots them out like a thick cloud (see Isa. 44:22, NKJV). He takes them off the record. We are made righteous and worthy in His eyes. Nothing Satan can say or do will change our position in Christ. And the Devil can take the joy out of the Christian life only when we allow him to.

It's important to distinguish between Satan's accusations and God's convictions. God convicts us in love; Satan accuses us in hatred. The Holy Spirit uses the Word to convict us; Satan uses feelings and memories to accuse us. When God convicts us, it draws us closer to Him; but when Satan accuses us, it pulls us away from the Lord. God's conviction leads to discipline and devotion. Satan's accusations lead to depression and discouragement. When God convicts, it is so we might look ahead and have hope. When Satan accuses, he wants us to look back and to give up.

Satan encourages us to accuse ourselves. Put on the breastplate of righteousness by faith and claim the righteousness of Christ. Your sins are forgiven. Your record is clean. The Lord ceases to remember your sins, and you should do likewise.

Others Accuse Us

A second tactic Satan loves to pull out of his bag of tricks is to cause other people to accuse us. I have noticed that everyone in the Bible who tried to serve the Lord was falsely accused. Nehemiah was accused of trying to become a king and to usurp the authority of others (see Neh. 6:6–7). David was accused of doing things he never did. In many of the psalms David prayed, 'Oh God, silence those liars. Silence those false accusers in Saul's court who are telling him lies about me.' Moses was accused of being a dictator. His own brother and sister accused him of trying to misuse his authority and lord it over everyone (see Num. 12).

In the New Testament we find the Apostle Paul being falsely accused. What was his attitude towards those accusations? 2 Corinthians 6:3, NKJV, says, 'We give no offense in anything, that our ministry may not be blamed.' Then Paul lists the types of difficulties he went through. How was he able to endure them? 'In purity, understanding … in truthful speech and in the power of God; with weapons of righteousness in the right hand and in the left' (vv. 6–7). Paul said, 'I have suffered many kinds of afflictions because many false charges have been brought against me. My enemies are telling all kinds of lies about me. But it makes no difference. I'm wearing the breastplate of righteousness. Let them accuse all they want to.'

And, of course, we can't forget how they falsely accused the Lord Jesus. He was accused of being a glutton and addicted to wine (see Matt. 11:19). They even called Him demon possessed (see Luke 11:14–19). But no doubt the greatest suffering He endured was during His last days on earth when He was arrested and false witnesses were called in to testify against Him. He was condemned to death on the charge of being a blasphemer (see Matt. 26:59–68). But the Lord Jesus Christ did not worry or fret about what they were saying because He knew the truth – that He was the very Son of God.

What can you do when other people accuse you? Turn to your intercessor, the Lord Jesus Christ. He is on your side and He will justify you:

> *What, then, shall we say in response to these things? If God is for us, who can be against us? … Who will bring any charge against those whom God has chosen? It is God who justifies. Who then is the one who condemns?*

> *No one. Christ Jesus who died – more than that, who was raised to life – is at the right hand of God and is also interceding for us. (Rom. 8:31, 33–34).*

When you are wearing the breastplate of righteousness, you know that your Intercessor is representing you before the throne of God.

Circumstances 'Accuse' Us

Satan encourages us to accuse ourselves. He encourages others to accuse us, and sometimes he even makes us believe that our circumstances are accusing us. We tell ourselves, *Oh, if only I was right with God, I wouldn't be going through this difficulty.* Satan makes us believe that God is punishing us for our sins by allowing us to suffer.

The life of Job is a prime example of Satan using circumstances to accuse a righteous person. Job's friends believed that his trials were the direct result of some sin in his life. They accused him again and again of hiding his sins (see Job 5:17; 8:1–6, 20–22; 11:1–20). They said, in effect, 'If the circumstances were different, we'd believe you Job; but what you are going through is proof that God is punishing you for your sins.'

We don't walk by sight; we walk by faith. We are wearing the breastplate of righteousness, and no matter what the circumstances may be, God will not forsake us. 'Who shall separate us from the love of Christ? Shall trouble or hardship or persecution or famine or nakedness or danger or sword? … No, in all these things we are more than conquerors through him who loved us' (Rom. 8:35,37). While some difficulties may be the result of our actions, God does not use these circumstances to punish us, nor does He desert us in our hour of need. When we feel that God doesn't care and that He is punishing us for some sin, Satan is working through our circumstances to accuse us. However, our trials can't defeat us if we remember who is on our side and use the breastplate of righteousness He has given us to protect our thoughts and emotions.

One of Satan's greatest weapons is false accusation. Whether the accusations are coming from other people, from our circumstances or from within ourselves, we need to remember that Satan has instigated them and that we have the breastplate of righteousness to defend ourselves against his attacks. By faith, continually put on this breastplate, remembering that you are wearing the righteousness of Jesus Christ and that His righteousness makes you accepted in the One He loves (see Eph. 1:6).

Chapter Five:

Blessed Are the Balanced

The Shoes of Peace

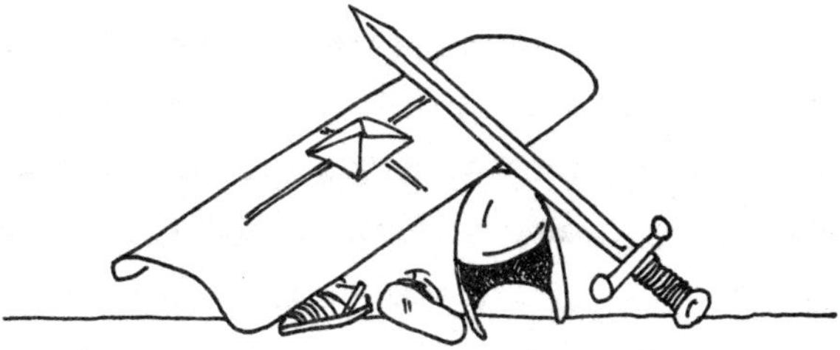

and with your feet fitted with the readiness that comes from the gospel of peace.

(Eph. 6:15)

In the war Satan is waging against us, we have seen the importance of standing firm against his onslaughts. We do this by relying on the strength and power of the Lord and by wearing the spiritual armour He has given us. In order to stand firm, we must have the right protection for our feet. Ephesians 6:14–15, NKJV, tells us what this protection is: 'Stand therefore, having … shod your feet with the preparation of the gospel of peace'.

In Paul's day, the Roman soldier wore sandals that were firmly fixed to his feet by leather thongs. On the soles of these sandals were hobnails to give the soldier a firm footing on the ground. This is the image painted by the Greek word translated 'preparation' (see v. 15). It means a firm footing, a strong foundation. A soldier knows that if he is having trouble with his feet, he cannot stand; and if he cannot stand, then he cannot fight well. Likewise, Christians need the firm footing that comes from standing on the Gospel of peace in order to keep their balance as they fight Satan.

What exactly is the Gospel that Paul was referring to in this passage? In 1 Corinthians 15:1–5, Paul defines it for us:

> *Now, brothers and sisters, I want to remind you of the gospel I preached to you, which you received and on which you have taken your stand. By this gospel you are saved, if you hold firmly to the word I preached to you. Otherwise, you have believed in vain. For what I received I passed on to you as of first importance: that Christ died for our sins according to the Scriptures, that he was buried, that he was raised on the third day according to the Scriptures, and that he appeared to Cephas, and then to the Twelve.*

Paul then goes on to list the various resurrection appearances of our Lord (see vv. 6–8).

The death, burial and resurrection of Christ, and the salvation He offers us, is the Gospel of peace that we firmly stand on. Satan hates this Gospel message because through it he has been defeated by Christ. Thus, he is continually trying to cause people to turn away from the Gospel and to preach some other Gospel. Paul warned the believers against falling into the trap of teaching or believing some other message. He exhorted them, 'Therefore, my dear brothers and sisters, stand firm. Let nothing move you. Always give yourselves fully to the work of the Lord, because you know that your labour in the Lord is not in vain' (v. 58). When it comes to serving the Lord, we should always be on the move and making progress. However, when it comes to the Gospel, we need to be unmovable and inflexible. We need to stand firmly on the *unchanging* Gospel, for it needs no improvement.

Throughout his letters Paul emphasised the importance of standing in the Gospel of the grace of God. In Romans 5:1–2 we learn that we can stand with God in peace because we have been justified by faith: 'Therefore, since we have been justified through faith, we have peace with God through our Lord Jesus Christ, through whom we have gained access by faith into this grace in which we now stand.'

In writing to the Galatians, Paul exhorted: 'It is for freedom that Christ has set us free. Stand firm, then, and do not let yourselves be burdened again by a yoke of slavery' (Gal. 5:1). Since we stand in the freedom of the Gospel, we should not allow Satan to again enslave us in the bondage of sinfulness.

Paul's strongest words about standing firmly on the only true Gospel are found in Galatians 1:6–8, where we read,

> *I am astonished that you are so quickly deserting the one who called you to live in the grace of Christ and are turning to a different gospel – which is really no gospel at all. Evidently some people are throwing you into confusion and are trying to pervert the gospel of Christ. But even if we or an angel from heaven should preach a gospel other than the one we preached to you, let them be under God's curse!*

We have only one Gospel, and we must be extremely careful to preach it exactly as God gave it to us, for we will be judged for what we teach.

Knowing the one true Gospel is paramount, for if you have a false Gospel, your beliefs about the Person of the Lord Jesus Christ – the only Son of God – will be wrong. If you are wrong on the Gospel, you will not understand the work of Jesus Christ and why He died. Likewise, your views of the needs of mankind will be erroneous. Christ died for our sins. Man is a sinner. The world needs to know the Gospel, the good news that no one has to stay the way he is. Jesus Christ has paid the price and has released the power that can transform lives. That is the Gospel.

As Christian soldiers, we have our feet shod with the preparation of the Gospel of peace. When we take our stand on the Gospel, God then gives us exactly what we need to defeat the Enemy and to hold our ground. Let's examine these shoes more closely and see what spiritual help they offer us for the war.

Stability

What does God give us when we wear the shoes of peace? First, He gives us *stability*. Many Christians in the world today are unstable. Paul was referring to these unstable people when he wrote: 'Then we will no longer be infants, tossed back and forth by the waves, and blown here and there by every wind of teaching and by the cunning and craftiness of people in their deceitful scheming' (Eph. 4:14).

Unstable people are not grounded in the Word of God. Like children, they believe everything they hear and are easily led astray because they don't know the truth of God's Word. Instability is a serious problem that can hinder – or destroy – our Christian life. For this reason, the Bible contains many warnings about being unstable. James tells us that a double-minded person is 'unstable in all they do' (Jas. 1:8). In Hebrews 13:9 we read, 'Do not be carried away by all kinds of strange teachings. It is good for our hearts to be strengthened by grace, not by eating ceremonial foods, which is of no benefit to those who do so.' In other words, don't believe one strange doctrine after another. Learn the Word of God and stand on the Gospel so you know exactly what you believe. Test every doctrine by the Person and work of the Lord Jesus Christ; otherwise, you will be tossed back and forth until you are finally carried away from God completely. A well-grounded understanding of the Word of God gives you stability so your faith will not be shaken.

People need to have confidence in life through competence in the Word of God. Many people know the television guide for the week, the batting averages of famous baseball players and many other titbits of trivia, but yet these same Christians don't even know the books of the Bible. When a problem arises, they have no idea where to look for a Scripture passage that can help them. How tragic!

Stability is one of the greatest needs among Christians today. Too many of God's people are tumbleweeds. They do not know the Word of God and thus are falling prey to all sorts of religious groups. They blow about from one group to another. They are wasting their time, energy and money on things that are not eternal.

The Gospel is the foundation of the Christian life, just as the feet support the entire weight of the body. No soldier would think of entering battle without his shoes on, because his feet need this vital protection if they are to give him stability and mobility. Likewise, we should continually wear the shoes of peace so that wherever we go, we are standing firmly on the Gospel. Then when other people try to blow our faith off course, we will have the stability we need to test what they say by the Word of God and to stand firm in our faith.

Balance

The shoes of the Gospel of peace not only give you stability but also give you *balance*. A soldier doesn't wear just one shoe into battle. To do so would throw off his balance and cause him to limp when he walked. He knows that he must have both shoes so that he can have a good footing and balance in battle.

Satan loves unbalanced Christians – those who concentrate so completely on one doctrine or practise of Scripture that they ignore its other teachings and what else God would have them do. Often I receive letters from people who accept a certain biblical doctrine and base their beliefs on that doctrine, while excluding many other teachings of Scripture. For example, someone may tell me that the Bible speaks only of election. He has forgotten Christ's invitation: 'let the one who wishes take the free gift of the water of life' (Rev. 22:17). On the other hand, someone else will write and say, 'Brother Wiersbe, I heard you talk about election. I don't find that in the Bible. The Bible just tells me that man should make a decision.' However, God's Word teaches both doctrines, and these doctrines need each other in order to be properly understood. Someone came to Charles Spurgeon one day and asked him how he reconciled predestination and man's free responsibility. Spurgeon wisely replied, 'I do not try to reconcile friends.'

In order to be balanced and able to walk as Christians, we need a thorough understanding of all the Bible's doctrines, teachings and commands. However, many believers are riding spiritual hobby horses. They are only concerned about one doctrine or activity in the church. For example, some people are very concerned about house to house visitation, but they have no interest in missions. For others, their only concern is their bus route. They have no interest in prayer. Still others are so busy fighting certain translations that they have no desire to see people receive the Word in their own language. While some activity or belief may be good in itself, if you try to divorce it from the rest of the Christian life, it can become destructive and useless.

When our faith is resting firmly on all the truths of the Gospel, we will have balance and stability in our Christian lives. This balance is vital if we are going to hold our ground against the Devil. When we begin to fight just one crusade, believing that we are doing the will of God, Satan will quickly move in. He will tear down our confidence in that belief or cause and then knock our spiritual feet out from under us. However, the Devil cannot move a Christian whose faith is resting in all of God's Word.

Mobility

The shoes of the Gospel give us not only the stability and balance we need to stand our ground in battle but also the *mobility* we need to fight. Even the best equipped and best protected soldier will likely be killed if he stands in one place for too long. He needs to be able to move so he can attack and can respond to the moves of the enemy.

The Roman soldier's hobnailed sandals were designed for mobility as well as for strength and protection. They were light enough for him to move and turn quickly. He was able to adjust and shift his position readily. They were comfortable so his feet didn't become tired and sore.

The problem in the Church today is that believers are standing still. They are not willing to move from their position. However, you don't wear shoes to stand still. Shoes were designed for walking and running. We wear the shoes of the Gospel, not just to stand our ground but to have the firm footing and mobility we need to respond to the tactics of the Enemy.

The one thing that is hindering the work of God most today is an *unwillingness* to change on the part of many Christians. This does not mean that we should change shoes. We must never change the Gospel. However, at times it is necessary to change our tactics and approach in sharing that good news.

Adaptability is important in fighting the Enemy. At Back to the Bible, we occasionally receive letters from people who are upset because we have made some minor changes to our methods. Sometimes it appears as if they believe that God set our methods in concrete when He began this ministry nearly 50 years ago. However, our founder, Theodore Epp, believed in change. He believed that while the message never changes, our methods for sharing that message must change in order to meet people where they are. The Devil frequently changes his approaches and adjusts his tactics, and unless we have the mobility to respond to these changes, he will quickly trample us underfoot.

Opportunity

When we take our stand on the Gospel of peace, God not only gives us stability, balance and mobility, but He also gives us *opportunity* for ministry. No soldier goes to war without knowing what he's fighting for. Likewise, as believers, we need to keep our goal in mind. Our goal in this battle is not merely to stand our ground and fight. We must also move forward to spread the Gospel. Many of the people who create problems in our lives are the people we need to reach with the Gospel.

Nothing gives us greater power for holy living than a readiness to share the Gospel. In Ephesians 6:15 the Greek word translated 'preparation' can also be translated 'readiness.' Have your feet shod 'with the preparation (readiness) of the gospel of peace'. The Apostle Peter reminded us that we should always be ready to witness for

Christ (see 1 Pet. 3:15). If we keep our shoes of peace on continually, we will be ready when the opportunity to witness comes.

Isn't it interesting that we are soldiers of peace in this battle? It is very important to remember who the Enemy is. Our adversary is the Devil – not people. We are ambassadors of reconciliation (see 2 Cor. 5:18–20), bringing a message of peace to the world. The Lord Jesus Christ came to earth to bring peace. The angels referred to it as 'on earth peace to those on whom his favour rests' (Luke 2:14). But He didn't just come to bring *peace* with Him, for 'he himself is our peace' (Eph. 2:14). He is able to establish peace between enemies. For example, He brought two enemies – the Jew and the Gentile – together into one Body, His Church (vv. 14–17). All people are at war with God, and it is our wonderful privilege to give them this Gospel of peace.

The feet that wear the shoes of peace are beautiful because they carry the message of peace. Isaiah 52:7 says, 'How beautiful on the mountains are the feet of those who bring good news, who proclaim peace, who bring good tidings'. The Apostle Paul quoted this verse in Romans 10 when he asked, 'How then shall they call on Him in whom they have not believed? And how shall they believe in Him of whom they have not heard? And how shall they hear without a preacher? And how shall they preach unless they are sent? As it is written: "How beautiful are the feet of those who preach the gospel of peace"' (vv. 14–15, NKJV).

Are you wearing the shoes of peace today? Do you exhibit a readiness to share the Gospel with others? God will give you the opportunity; it's your responsibility to be ready. The kind of soldier who will be victorious on the battlefield is the one who is stable and balanced, who has good mobility and who uses every opportunity to share the good news of the Gospel. If you have the shoes of peace strapped to your feet, you will be this kind of soldier.

Chapter Six:

Put Out the Fires

The Shield of Faith

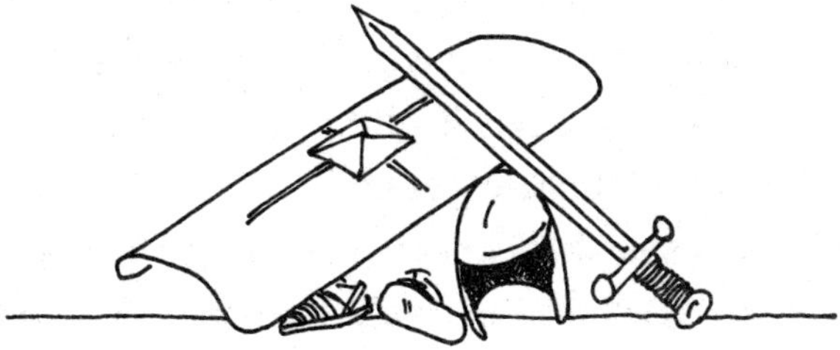

In addition to all this, take up the shield of faith, with which you can extinguish all the flaming arrows of the evil one.

(Eph. 6:16)

Our Enemy has a well-stocked arsenal of weapons with which to wage war against us. His quiver is full of flaming arrows of adversity, and he constantly bombards our defences with these fiery darts. Frequently he fires a round of problems at us (sickness, financial loss, broken relationships) and then when our defences are down, he hits us with his emotional darts of anger, fear, doubt, depression or self-pity. Without a strong line of defence, these arrows will hit their mark, and we will fall on the battlefield.

But the Lord has given us a shield to ward off these flaming arrows – the shield of faith: 'above all, taking the shield of faith with which you will be able to quench all the fiery darts of the wicked one' (Eph. 6:16, NKJV).

The shield that Paul was referring to here was not the small, round shield we normally think of. He was referring to the shield that a Roman soldier carried. These shields were quite large (almost like a door) – usually about two feet by four feet. By crouching behind it, the soldier could hide himself completely. The shield was made of wood that was covered with cloth and leather. Sometimes the soldier would dip it in water so that the fire-tipped arrows would be extinguished when they struck the shield.

Paul used the image of this kind of shield to represent the believer's faith. What kind of faith was the apostle referring to? He was not talking about a historical faith that says, 'Oh, I believe all the historical facts of the Bible. I believe that Jesus lived and died and rose again from the dead.' He was not even talking about saving faith, although this kind of faith is vital. Paul was speaking of a practical, everyday faith that says, 'I will not rely on myself or on my experience or my knowledge. Instead, I'm trusting God to give me the victory today.' This kind of faith is what overcomes Satan and his forces. 'This is the victory that has overcome the world, even our faith' (1 John 5:4).

It Protects the Soldier

Satan's bow is drawn and ready to shoot his fiery darts at us when we least expect it. We must continually be prepared to ward off his attacks. What special help does the shield of faith give us as we seek to stand our ground and to hold our inheritance in Jesus Christ? First, the shield of faith protects the soldier.

Satan's fiery darts are swift and silent. We receive no advance warning of their arrival.

Suddenly, the flaming arrows land, and we feel a slight tinge of pain. Then, before we know it, a raging fire breaks out, destroying everything in its path. The Devil throws these darts at us. He waits and watches closely. Then, when our lives are going well and we stop relying on the Lord's help, Satan strikes us when our shields are down.

Satan's Fiery Darts

What are the fiery darts that Satan hurls our way? Satan throws many different kinds of darts at us. We must be careful not to allow these fiery darts to penetrate our souls. For once they do, they will catch fire and do great damage.

One of Satan's deadly darts is the dart of *fear*. We all struggle with fear at times. Often during a normal and uneventful day, we can suddenly become afraid. This can be triggered by something someone says to us, by a change in circumstances, by a letter we read, by a telephone call, by news we hear on the radio or television. Whatever the source, we are suddenly gripped by fear. If we allow this fear to linger, it soon spreads like wildfire and begins to destroy our faith.

Faith and fear do not live in the same heart. When we become afraid, we lose our faith in the Lord's ability to help us. When a fierce storm arose at sea, the disciples were terrified. They awakened Jesus, who was asleep in the boat. After calming the storm, Jesus asked them, 'Why are you afraid? Where is your faith? Didn't you trust Me to take care of you?' (see Mark 4:35–40).

Satan's second type of fiery dart is the dart of *doubt*. We begin to have doubts about God. We ask ourselves, *Does God really know what He is doing? Does He understand what my problems are? Is His Word really true?* It is amazing how people can read the Bible all of their lives and then at a certain point say, 'You know, I don't believe that.' Satan works in us, planting these doubts, until we begin to question even the basic tenets of our faith.

In addition to doubts about what the Bible teaches, Satan also tries to throw doubts about other people at us. We become sceptical about fellow believers in the church. We begin to question: *Does she really like me? Is he really qualified to be serving the Lord? What did he really mean by that statement in the sermon?* Satan fans these fires of doubt, and before long, they grow and multiply until they destroy our faith and our relationships with others.

Besides planting doubts about God and about others in our minds, Satan loves to cause us to have doubts about ourselves. Of course, we should not be overly confident in ourselves, for then we are guilty of the sin of pride. But we need to guard against having doubts about our salvation and our Christian life. The Lord does want us to examine our hearts frequently, saying, 'Search me, God, and know my heart; test me and know my anxious thoughts' (Ps. 139:23). We need this soul searching at times to rid ourselves of sin that has crept in (see v. 24). But this can become dangerous when we dwell on the faults we find and begin to fan the flames of doubt instead of trusting God to help us.

Sometimes Satan's fiery darts are *words*. He uses words against us in many ways. Often these darts invade our thoughts so that filthy or slanderous words come to mind. Words of criticism and hatred form there, often spilling out into our speech. Satan likes to throw these words at our mind, and we start to think things we really don't want to think. Or sometimes he throws these darts at our will, and we suddenly decide we are going to do something we know we should not do. Sometimes he throws the darts at our conscience, and we start feeling dirty and sinful inside.

A fourth fiery dart Satan frequently uses is the dart of *confusion*. When we find our thinking, emotions or lives becoming confused, we immediately know that Satan is the cause, 'For God is not the author of confusion' (1 Cor. 14:33, NKJV). We need to resist the Devil's efforts to confuse us by relying on the peace and strength of the Lord.

None of us want to be the target of Satan's fiery darts of fear, doubt, words and confusion. The first step to ridding ourselves of these darts is to identify the source of our feelings. We can always tell the fiery darts of the Wicked One from the inward temptations of our own nature because Satan's darts hit suddenly and without warning, spreading quickly. When our minds are suddenly filled with these fears, doubts or words, we initially resist them, saying,

'Where did that come from? I don't usually think like this.' When this happens, we need to immediately ask God for the strength to dispel these thoughts from our minds by using the shield of faith.

Faith's Firm Shield

The shield of faith protects us in two ways. First, it stops the fiery darts so they don't injure us. Then it puts out the fire so the damage doesn't spread.

What kind of faith was Paul referring to when he described the shield of faith? He was not talking about a faith in ourselves or in the doctrines we believe, but faith in God, who is our shield.

This faith in God manifests itself in three ways. First, we have faith in God's person. We not only believe that He exists but that He is actively involved in our lives. After Abraham had returned from rescuing Lot, the Lord told him in a vision, 'Do not be afraid, Abram. I am your shield, your very great reward' (Gen. 15:1). God is our shield (protection) and our great reward (provision). He is all we need.

When he was experiencing trouble, David knew he could trust the Lord to shield him. He stated, 'Lord, how many are my foes! How many rise up against me! Many are saying of me, "God will not deliver him." But you, Lord, are a shield around me, my glory, the One who lifts my head high. I call out to the Lord, and he answers me from his holy mountain' (Ps. 3:1–4). God hears us when we cry out to Him and will shield us when we have faith in him.

Our faith is not only in God's person but also in God's *promises*. Romans 10:17 tells us, 'faith comes from hearing the message, and the message is heard through the word about Christ.' The Word of God contains God's promises and answers for every problem we face. However, when Satan is aiming his fiery darts at us, we often begin to doubt God's promises. We must remember that the Lord has never once failed to keep one of His good promises (see 1 Kings 8:56). God has told us in His Word that He will help us, and we can trust Him to keep His Word!

We also have faith in God's *providence*. This is the kind of faith that says, 'we know that in all things God works for the good of those who love him' (Rom. 8:28). Does this mean we can deliberately sin and expect God to use it for good? No, it means that no matter what kind of battle we may be in, God is always in control and will protect His faithful soldiers.

It Protects the Armour

Besides protecting the soldier, the shield of faith also protects the rest of the armour. You may be asking yourself, *Why do I need to protect the armour? If I'm wearing the helmet of salvation, the breastplate of righteousness, the belt of truth and the shoes of peace and am carrying the sword of the Spirit, isn't that enough to protect me?* No, Ephesians 6:16, NKJV, says, 'above all (you take) the shield of faith'. The words 'above all' mean that faith is of paramount importance. The other parts of the armour won't function properly apart from faith. When you put on the belt of truth, you are placing your faith in the God of truth. When you put on the breastplate of righteousness, it shows that you have faith that your God is holy, righteous and just. When you put on the shoes of peace, you have faith in the Gospel. And as we shall see, the helmet of salvation, the sword of the Spirit, and prayer all depend on faith. 'Without faith it is impossible to please God' (Heb. 11:6).

Faith is vital to the Christian life. That's why Satan attacks your faith. He will do everything he can to keep you from the Word of God. He will try to make you worry about everything that happens, especially all the changes going on around you that you don't understand. He wants to make you confused so that you lose your confidence in God.

The shield of faith is out in front to protect the rest of the armour. When it is properly in place, 'you will be able to quench all the fiery darts of the wicked one' (Eph. 6:16, NKJV). Notice the word 'all'. Satan has no tactic, no strategy, no fiery dart to throw at you that God cannot equip you to defeat. You need to remember that you are on the winning side.

It Unites the Soldiers

Not only does the shield of faith protect the soldier and the rest of the armour, but it also unites the soldiers in the army. 'How could it do that?' you ask. Well, the edges of those big shields were bevelled in such a way that they could be locked together. A row of Roman soldiers could put their shields together to form a solid wall. Swords and arrows couldn't penetrate that wall as they marched forward.

This is a beautiful illustration of what faith should mean to you and me. Because of our common bond of faith in the Lord Jesus, you and I should love each other, walk together, stand together and fight together against our Enemy. But the sad truth is that too often we spend all of our energy fighting with, or competing with, each other. We have no energy left to combat our true Enemy. Churches today are too busy bragging about their shields and polishing their shields to actually use them! Just think of what God could accomplish in this world if every believer would stand with his shield united with his neighbour's in one great wall of faith! This is what the Apostle Paul envisioned when he wrote, 'until we all reach unity in the faith and in the knowledge of the Son of God' (Eph. 4:13).

We are all trying to fight our own battle and to do it our own way. I appreciate what the Apostle Peter wrote in 1 Peter 5:8–9: 'Be alert and of sober mind. Your enemy the devil prowls around like a roaring lion looking for someone to devour. Resist him, standing firm in the faith, because you know that the family of believers throughout the world is undergoing the same kind of sufferings.' Peter was saying, 'Don't think you are fighting that lion by yourself. Don't even try to defeat him yourself. Move close to the other soldiers, and lock your shields together. Don't let any division be found in the ranks, and then God will give you victory.' We need unity among believers today. If we would all pray and trust God together, we would accomplish much more. But we become selfish, individualistic and proud. We don't want to stand or work together.

When we face Satan and his army on the battlefield, we'd better be certain that we have the shield of faith. It is our best protection against Satan's fiery darts. It not only protects us and the rest of our armour, but it also unites us with our fellow soldiers. What a privileged people we are to be able to wear the whole armour of God – but especially to have the shield of faith.

Chapter Seven:

Think Like a Soldier!

The Helmet of Salvation

Take the helmet of salvation and the sword of the Spirit, which is the word of God.

(Eph. 6:17)

In a war the two most sought-after – and most vulnerable – targets are the heart and the head. If a soldier is wounded in either of these places, he will likely die. For this reason, a helmet has always been one of the most important pieces of the soldier's equipment.

The same is true for the Christian soldier. In Ephesians 6:17 we are commanded to 'Take the helmet of salvation'. The Roman soldier had a bronze helmet with a leather strap on it. He carried this helmet over his shoulder or on his belt until he needed to put it on for the battle. The helmet never left the soldier's side, and he never entered the battle without first putting his helmet on.

What is the purpose of the helmet of salvation? It protects your mind from the attacks of the Enemy. Salvation involves your mind. In order to be saved, a person must first repent. Thus, repentance is a vital part of the Gospel message. John the Baptist, in preparing the way for the Lord's ministry, cried out, 'Repent, for the kingdom of heaven has come near' (Matt. 3:2). Likewise, our Lord preached the same message of repentance (see 4:17). Paul also preached repentance towards God and faith in the Lord Jesus Christ (see Acts 20:21).

What is repentance? It is a change of mind. This involves more than merely looking back at something we did in the past and regretting that it happened or that we were caught. Sincere repentance is not just a feeling of regret or self-pity. We change our minds completely about our sins and what God has to say about them. We not only hate the fact that we sinned, but we also hate the sins themselves. With this change of mind comes a change of life. The Christian life must begin with both repentance and faith.

Our Christian lives continue to grow as we cultivate our knowledge of the Word of God. 'But grow in the grace and knowledge of our Lord and Saviour Jesus Christ' (2 Pet. 3:18). A person who does not use his mind is not going to grow mentally or spiritually. God wants us to have a spiritual mind – the mind of our Lord Jesus Christ (see Phil. 2:5). He wants our minds to be transformed: 'be transformed by the renewing of your mind' (Rom. 12:2).

And so the Christian life begins with repentance – a change of mind – and faith in Christ. It grows as our mind is transformed. We will not have victory in the Christian life unless we have an understanding of the Word of God, of how Satan works and of how God gives us the victory. We must know Satan's tactics. Paul stated in 2 Corinthians 2:11, 'we are not unaware of his schemes.' But unfortunately many Christians are ignorant of his schemes. They don't realise that they are walking right into the trap Satan has set for them.

In order to grow and have victory in the Christian life, something has to happen to our minds. However, some believers only emphasise the emotions. They want to have a glorious time feeling good. But feelings come and go. Sometimes our closest walk with the Lord comes at a time when we aren't feeling very good or very victorious. Other believers emphasise only the will. They say that no matter how we feel, we must be fulfilling a certain list of requirements at all times. But, in reality, the Christian life is a combination of all three. The mind is enlightened. The heart is stirred. The will is enabled to do what God wants us to do. Only when the mind, the heart and the will are working together can we serve the Lord effectively. Therefore, we can't ignore the helmet of salvation. We must prepare our minds before we enter the battle or Satan will deceive us and defeat us.

To Prevent a Divided Mind

Some Christians are not experiencing victory in their lives because they do not have the right mindset. They have not put on the helmet of salvation; therefore, they are not thinking like a Christian. When we put on the helmet of salvation, God communicates His thoughts to us through His Word and by His Holy Spirit. If we are wearing the helmet of salvation, we will not have the wrong kinds of thoughts and attitudes.

What wrong attitudes and thoughts are averted by wearing the helmet of salvation? One of the most important functions of the helmet is to prevent a *divided mind*. A soldier who has a divided mind will never win the battle, for such a person is 'unstable in all they do' (Jas. 1:8). We wear the shoes of peace in order to have stability in our stand and walk with the Lord. But what good are the shoes of the Gospel of peace if our mind is divided? We cannot take a half-hearted approach to the Christian life. If our loyalties and thoughts are divided, our lives will be unsteady. We cannot ride the fence without eventually falling.

The Lord Jesus cannot tolerate lukewarm Christians. In Revelation 3:15–16 He told the

Church of Laodicea, 'you are neither cold nor hot. I wish you were either one or the other! So, because you are lukewarm – neither hot nor cold – I am about to spit you out of my mouth.' In other words, if we are not willing to enter the battle wholeheartedly for Him, then He would prefer that we didn't join His forces at all. We must choose sides. This is what Moses told the Israelites. He said, 'Whoever is for the LORD, come to me' (Ex. 32:26). Later, Joshua again warned the people that they couldn't serve both God and idols. He said, 'choose for yourselves this day whom you will serve … . But as for me and my household, we will serve the LORD' (Josh. 24:15). We can serve only one master. Jesus stated, 'Whoever is not with me is against me, and whoever does not gather with me scatters' (Luke 11:23). Either we are completely on the Lord's side or we are against Him. There is no middle ground on the Christian battlefield.

We need a mindset of victory. What kind of a mindset is this? Peter described it for us in 1 Peter 4:1: 'Therefore, since Christ suffered in his body, arm yourselves also with the same attitude, because whoever suffers in the body has finished with sin.' Our mind is a weapon in this battle. We must arm ourselves with the same attitude towards sin and suffering that Jesus had. The Lord did not have a divided mind. He had a single purpose in life – to glorify God and accomplish His will. In order to have this same attitude, the believer does 'not live the rest of their earthly lives for evil human desires, but rather for the will of God' (v. 2).

The Bible gives us numerous examples of soldiers of God who armed themselves with the right mind – Joshua and Caleb for instance. In Numbers 13 Moses sent 12 spies into Canaan to survey the situation. Ten of the spies had divided minds. Instead of looking only to the Lord as their source of strength, they began comparing themselves with their huge and powerful enemies. They said, 'We can't conquer these people. They are giants. Their cities have tall walls around them. We are like grasshoppers compared to them' (see vv. 28, 31–33). Joshua and Caleb were the only two spies who said, 'We should go up and take possession of the land, for we can certainly do it' (v. 30). Because their minds weren't divided, these two men faithfully took God at His word. They trusted Him to give them the land as He had promised.

David is another example. He was able to face the giant Goliath without fear because he was wearing the helmet of salvation. His mind was focused only on the victory. He refused to wear Saul's armour and use his sword because he trusted God's protection and power completely. David told the giant, 'You come against me with sword and spear and javelin, but I come against you in the name of the LORD Almighty, ... whom you have defied. This day the LORD will deliver you into my hands' (1 Sam. 17:45–46). David faced Goliath with a single mind centred on victory.

The Devil wants us to have a divided mind. He wants us to look in two directions at the same time – towards heaven and towards earth – because then he can trip us up. We must constantly guard against having divided minds and loyalties. Since we have risen with Christ, 'set your hearts on things above, where Christ is, seated at the right hand of God' (Col. 3:1).

To Prevent a Deceived Mind

Not only does the helmet of salvation protect us

from a divided mind, but it also prevents us from having a *deceived mind*.

The Devil is the great deceiver. We read in 2 Corinthians 11:3, NKJV: 'But I fear, lest somehow, as the serpent deceived Eve by his craftiness, so your minds may be corrupted from the simplicity that is in Christ.' That word 'simplicity' refers to a single-hearted devotion. You see, a divided mind leads to a deceived mind. If we do not have a single-hearted devotion to the Lord Jesus Christ, Satan will be able to deceive our minds, just as he deceived Eve's in the Garden of Eden.

How did Satan deceive the mind of Eve? Genesis 3 gives us the answer to that question. He took three very simple steps in deceiving her. First, he *questioned God's word*: 'He said to the woman, 'Did God really say, "You must not eat from any tree in the garden"?' (v. 1). Then he *denied God's word*: '"You will not certainly die," the snake said to the woman' (v. 4). Finally, Satan *substituted his own lie in place of God's word*: 'For God knows that when you eat from it your eyes will be opened, and you will be like God, knowing good and evil' (v. 5). Satan follows these same three steps in deceiving us today.

Satan is able to divide our minds and deceive us if we put down our helmet of salvation for even one moment. Joshua found this out. When the Gibeonites heard of the Israelites' victories at Jericho and Ai, they feared for their lives. So they devised a plan to trick the Children of Israel into making a treaty with them (see Josh. 9). They put on old, dirty clothes and worn-out shoes and packed some mouldy bread in their sacks. Then they walked to the Israelites' camp and said they had come from a great distance. Rather than asking for the Lord's counsel, Joshua believed their story and made a covenant with them. This covenant caused the Israelites all kinds of trouble. Joshua momentarily took off his helmet, and Satan was able to deceive him. If Joshua had been wearing the helmet of salvation, he would not have hesitated to pray and seek the mind of the Lord about how to handle this situation. But he had laid aside his helmet.

Peter made the same mistake. In Matthew 16:16 he made his great confession of faith in Christ. He obviously had his helmet on. Then Jesus began to teach His disciples that He was going to suffer and die. But Peter had now laid aside his helmet, for he said, 'Never, Lord!... This shall never happen to you!' (v. 22). Therefore, Jesus said to Peter, 'Get behind me, Satan. You are a stumbling-block to me. You are not thinking like God, you are thinking like a man' (see v. 23). Satan found it easy to deceive Peter because he didn't have his helmet on.

One reason why it's so important for us to study the Word of God is so that Satan cannot deceive us. If we know the truth, we won't be such easy prey for Satan's lies. While it's good to study subjects such as how to raise your children or how to handle your money, you need to know what God says about these areas. God's truth is foundational. You need to measure what everyone else says about these topics by the truth of God's Word. The better you know the Word of God, the better you'll be able to raise your family or handle your business affairs.

To Prevent a Doubtful Mind

Satan loves to deceive us; but if you're wearing the helmet of salvation, you will not have a divided mind, a deceived mind or a *doubtful mind*. In Luke 12:29 the Lord Jesus warned, 'Neither be ye of doubtful mind' (KJV). In other words, don't let your mind be filled with doubts. This is the only place in the New Testament where this Greek word is used. The Greek word translated 'doubtful' gives us our English word 'meteor'. This word means 'to be raised on high, to be in mid-air, to live in suspense, to hover'.

Many Christians have minds that are living in suspense or are hovering; they never settle down to anything. They're always up in the air about something. They worry about yesterday, today and tomorrow. They're never sure whether to believe this teacher or that one. They have minds filled with doubts.

Why is it wrong to have a doubtful mind? Because God provides for us and protects us. And how Satan loves for us not to believe that! If we have a doubtful mind, we won't claim God's promises. If we don't claim God's promises, we can't enjoy God's power. If we don't enjoy God's power, we can't share in His victory. And then Satan can rejoice over our defeat. Make sure you wear your helmet of salvation or Satan will trip you up with a mind full of doubts.

To Prevent a Discouraged Mind

Along with these doubts, Satan tries to fill our minds with discouragement. But the helmet of salvation can help prevent a *discouraged mind*. In writing about the spiritual armour in another place, Paul describes the helmet's power over discouragement: 'But since we belong to the day, let us be sober, putting on faith and love as a breastplate, and the hope of salvation as a helmet' (1 Thess. 5:8).

The helmet of salvation is the hope of salvation. When a soldier loses his hope, he loses the battle. If he looks around and says, 'We cannot possibly win,' he will give up and will then be defeated. Defeat comes from within – not from without. The successful Christian soldier is the one who never capitulates inside. Within his heart he continually says, 'I know that God is going to see me through.' True hope in the Christian life is not a 'hope so' attitude. It is a firm and unwavering confidence in God's promises and purposes.

What creates discouragement in the Christian battle? Discouragement comes when we forget the blessed hope we have in Christ (see Titus 2:13). We forget that the Pioneer of our salvation is coming to save us and to take us to glory (see Heb. 2:10). We start walking by sight and not by faith. As we look around and see casualties and chaos everywhere, we say, 'There's no sense in going any farther.' We give in to our feelings and quit.

So many Christians today are giving in to their feelings. They say, 'I don't feel like praying or reading God's Word today.' But this is when we need most to pray and read God's Word. Others say, 'I don't feel like going to church.' But these are the times when we need to be with God's people. When we begin to succumb to our feelings, then we start listening to what other people have to say. Before long, our minds and spirits are discouraged. When we take off the helmet of salvation, we cannot lift our heads high. Instead, we hang our heads in discouragement and defeat. The solution to our discouragement is allowing God to lift up our head and firmly place the helmet of salvation back on it.

If we are wearing the helmet of salvation, we can then take our stand. Satan will not be able to invade our minds and rob us of the inheritance that we have in Jesus Christ. The Enemy is continually using his weapons of division, deception, doubt and discouragement against us. However, when we make up our minds to fight the battle to the very end, Satan will be unable to divide our thoughts and loyalties. When we believe God's truth without exception, the Devil can't deceive us. When we claim the Lord's promises and rejoice in the hope of our salvation, we will not be plagued by doubts and discouragement. By having the mind of the Lord Jesus Christ, a transformed mind, one day we will have the privilege of trading in our helmet for a crown.

Chapter Eight:

Spiritual Swordsmanship

The Sword of the Spirit

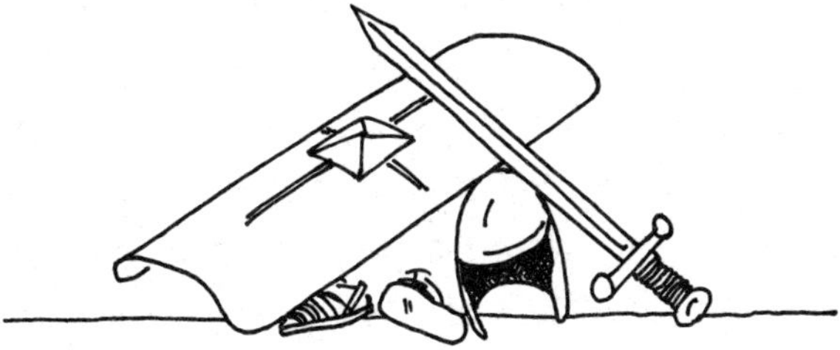

Take the helmet of salvation and the sword of the Spirit, which is the word of God.

(Eph. 6:17)

While armour is absolutely necessary for the protection of the soldier, the warrior would be ineffective in battle if he had no weapon with which to attack the enemy and to defend himself.

Likewise, the Christian soldier must have a weapon for his war against Satan. And God has indeed given us a very powerful weapon – the sword of the Spirit. 'Take ... the sword of the Spirit, which is the word of God' (Eph. 6:17).

It is interesting that God compares His Word to a sword. The sword that Paul was referring to here was a short, straight sword that was used for close combat by the Roman soldier. Satan doesn't stop with just throwing fiery darts at us. Sometimes he and his army move in on us, and we are forced to do hand-to-hand combat with them. The only way to resist them is by attacking with the sword of the Spirit – the Word of God. The Bible promises that when we resist the Devil, he will flee from us (see Jas. 4:7).

Maybe you are saying, 'Well, I believe the Bible, I study God's Word regularly and try to apply it to my everyday life. Yet I am still defeated at times. Why?' Perhaps you are trying to use the sword by itself. God wants us to use the sword, but He wants us to use it in conjunction with the other provisions He has made for victory. We can't separate the sword from these other provisions.

The Sword and the Spirit

In using the Word of God to defeat the Devil, we must take several precautions in order to use this weapon effectively. First, we must *be careful not to separate the sword from the Holy Spirit of God*. Notice that Ephesians 6:17 describes God's Word as 'the sword of the Spirit'. The Bible was inspired by the Holy Spirit. It was given to us through the ministry of the Holy Spirit (see 2 Pet. 1:21). The Holy Spirit is the One who teaches us the Word of God (see John 14:26) and who guides us into all truth (see 16:13). It is the Holy Spirit who reminds us of what we have learned and who enables us to practise what He has taught us (see 14:26). The Bible is a remarkable book. It is the only book in the world where the author is immediately available to guide us in understanding it as we read it. It is the only book in the world that when you attempt to practise its teachings, the author is there to give you the strength and grace you need.

The Holy Spirit of God gave us the sword of the Spirit; therefore, we must be careful to depend on the Spirit as we use the Word of God. The problem today is that too many Christians acquire a great deal of Bible knowledge and think that this knowledge alone will defeat Satan. However, Satan knows the Bible better than we do. He can, and often does, deceive people by using the Word of God. We read in 2 Corinthians 10:4–5: 'The weapons we fight with are not the weapons of the world. On the contrary, they have divine power to demolish strongholds. We demolish arguments and every pretension that sets itself up against the knowledge of God'. We are in a spiritual battle, not fighting against flesh and blood; therefore, simply quoting Scripture is not enough. The Devil can quote the Word. He used it in tempting Jesus (see Matt. 4:6). The Pharisees quoted Scripture to the Lord Jesus. Unbelievers can quote Bible verses. No, we need the power of the Holy Spirit to enable us to claim the Word of God and then practise it.

We are in a spiritual fight; only a spiritual weapon will be effective in this warfare. Hebrews 4:12–13 tells us, 'For the word of God is alive and active. Sharper than any double-edged sword, it penetrates even to dividing soul and spirit, joints and marrow; it judges the thoughts and attitudes of the heart. Nothing in all creation is hidden from God's sight. Everything is uncovered and laid bare before the eyes of him to whom we must give account.' The Word of God is a spiritual sword – not a material one. A material sword becomes dull; the Word of God never loses its sharpness. While the hearers or the preachers may be dull (see Heb. 5:11), the Bible never is.

Unlike a sword, which is powerless without the hand of the swordsman, the Word contains its own power. This is a spiritual power that 'penetrates even to dividing soul and spirit' (4:12). God's Word is a discerner, a critic and a judge. It reveals what is in the human heart. Only the Holy Spirit can know the thoughts and intentions lying within us and can convict us of our sins by using the Word. Thus, without the Holy Spirit, the sword loses much of its power.

Being able to quote the Bible is not enough. We must also read the Word daily, understand it, and know what it teaches. We should memorise and meditate on it. Most importantly, we should obey it. The Lord gave Joshua success because he was faithful in meditating on and obeying the book of the Law (see Josh. 1:8). In order for the sword of the Spirit to manifest its power in us, it must first be an integral part of our lives. We can't separate the sword from the Holy Spirit.

The Sword and the Other Armour

Just as we can't separate the sword from the Holy Spirit, *neither can we separate it from the rest of the armour*. Of course, we can carry the sword but not wear the armour, or we can wear the armour and not use the sword. However, without both the protection of the armour and the power of the sword, we leave ourselves open to attack.

Notice in the description of the armour in Ephesians 6 that the sword of the Spirit is sixth on the list. This indicates to me that the Word of God is an integral part of the total picture. It's not enough to walk around with our Bible. We must also have the belt of truth – integrity. I have met people in my ministry who can quote and defend the Bible, but they have no integrity. They can't be trusted. They have given themselves, and Christ, a bad name. Without integrity, no one will listen to what we have to say when we use the sword. Likewise, if we aren't wearing the breastplate of righteousness – if we don't claim by faith the righteousness of Jesus Christ – the Word of God cannot work in our lives. If the shoes of the Gospel of peace are not on our feet – if we are not standing firm on the Gospel – our attempts to share the good news are not going to be too effective. The same is true for the shield of faith and the helmet of the hope of salvation. All the parts of the armour work together. A soldier does not wear one piece of armour one day and then take it off and put on another the next. Neither does he dress for battle and then leave his sword at home. The soldier of Christ must have on the whole armour of God. Every part must be in place if he is to stand against the Enemy.

Don't try to separate the sword from the rest of the armour. While studying the Word of God is good, it is also good to let the Word of God study us. The Word is a window that reveals God and His world to us. But it is also a mirror that shows us as we really are. We should examine our armour in the mirror of the Word and ask ourselves, *Am I really living as I should?* As Christian soldiers, we are carrying the sword of the Spirit. But if the Holy Spirit is grieved because of our lack of integrity or our unwillingness to witness or our doubt, unbelief or discouragement, how can the sword of the Spirit be effective in our life?

The Sword and Prayer

We are not to separate the sword of the Word from the Holy Spirit or from the rest of the armour. Furthermore, *we cannot separate the sword of the Spirit from prayer*. This is quite evident from the passage in Ephesians 6: 'Take ... the sword of the Spirit, which is the word of God.... And pray in the Spirit on all occasions' (vv. 17–18). We also know from other passages of Scripture that the Word of God and prayer are inseparable. The early Church leaders gave themselves 'to prayer and the ministry of the word' (Acts 6:4). The Lord Jesus Christ promised His disciples, 'If you remain in me and my words (the Word of God) remain in you, ask whatever you wish (prayer), and it will be done for you' (John 15:7). We could give many other references where the Word of God and prayer are linked together in the Scriptures. It is not hard to understand why. The Word of God enlightens us, while prayer enables us. God's

Word reveals the will of God; prayer enables us to do that will. We cannot expect to have our prayers answered unless we pray in God's will, and we know God's will because He has revealed it to us in His Word.

Exodus 17 contains a beautiful illustration of how the Word of God and prayer work together. The nation of Israel had been delivered from the land of Egypt, and God was meeting all their needs. But then the Amalekites came against the Israelites to do battle. Exodus 17:9–11 says:

> *Moses said to Joshua, 'Choose some of our men and go out to fight the Amalekites. Tomorrow I will stand on top of the hill with the staff of God in my hands.' So Joshua fought the Amalekites as Moses had ordered, and Moses, Aaron and Hur went to the top of the hill. As long as Moses held up his hands, the Israelites were winning, but whenever he lowered his hands, the Amalekites were winning.*

Because Moses' arms became tired, he sat down on a rock while Aaron and Hur held his arms up. The Israelites then prevailed and won the battle. This is an illustration of how God's Word (symbolised by Joshua's sword) and prayer (symbolised by Moses' rod) worked together. The sword down in the valley in Joshua's hands would have done very little good without prayer, but prayer up on the hilltop would have done very little good without the use of the army. Our battle against Satan requires the use of both the Word of God and prayer.

I wonder if we don't have too much Bible and not enough intercession today. Now I know that some churches don't give enough attention to God's Word. Even some Christians spend only a minimal amount of time reading and studying their Bibles. But I think too often we concentrate more on the Bible than on prayer. We need to combine preaching with praying, combine instruction with intercession and combine studies with supplication. Don't separate the sword from prayer.

The Sword and Praise

Finally, *don't separate the sword from praise.* The Word of God and praise go together, just as the

Word of God and prayer go together. Psalm 149:6 is one verse that indicates this: 'May the praise of God be in their mouths and a double-edged sword in their hands'. That would be an interesting choir! Imagine what you would think next Sunday if your choir walked into their seats carrying swords – literal swords! Psalm 149 pictures a singing army. Do you know why? Because God wins victories through our praise.

We find an illustration of this concept in 2 Chronicles 20. The Moabites, the Ammonites and the Edomites all invaded Judah, and Jehoshaphat (the king) was facing the battle of his life. So he sought the Lord's will through prayer. God responded to him through Jahaziel, 'Don't be afraid of this multitude. The battle is not yours but Mine. You won't need to fight, but you will see the victory' (see vv. 15–17). Upon hearing this, the Levites praised the Lord 'with a very loud voice' (v. 19). How were the people of Judah able to win this war without fighting? In what seems to us a highly unusual tactic, Jehoshaphat put the choir out in front of the army (see v. 21)! The choir began to praise the Lord in anticipation of the truth of

His word. And as they did so, the enemy was defeated (see v. 22).

The praise of Jehoshaphat's choir must have been quite different from our worship and praise. Much of our praise today sounds as if we belong to the Enemy rather than having a triumphant ring of victory. Do you know why our praise is losing much of its power? Because it's not tied to the Word of God (see Heb. 4:12). That's why I rejoice to see the increase in the use of songs based on Scripture. Too many of our songs today have no connection with the sword in our hands. So many of our songs do not praise God; they praise the singer or talk about some problem in life.

'May the praise of God be in their mouths and a double-edged sword in their hands' (Ps. 149:6). Don't separate the Word of God from praise. When Jehoshaphat and his choir went out to praise God, they won the victory. Prayer changes things, but praise also changes things because it reminds us to trust the One who can give us victory.

The Word of God that we teach should be related to the praise that we sing. Our songs should be based on the Word of the Living God. Our music should edify rather than entertain. Music should not be a filler: it should encourage people to worship God. If you say you are a Bible student, then you ought to love your hymnbook. The hymnbook puts 'the praise of God' in your mouth, while the Bible puts the 'double-edged sword' in your hand.

We must use the sword of the Spirit in conjunction with the other provisions the Lord has given us for victory. We must not separate it from the Holy Spirit, for He will guide us in our use of the Word of God. We must not separate it from the rest of the armour. Unless we are wearing all of the armour, the sword will not be effective. We must not separate it from prayer or from praise. Both prayer and praise must accompany our use of the Word of God to ensure victory. Just as it takes a soldier time to become accustomed to using his sword and to appreciate its usefulness, it will take us a lifetime to become acquainted with all of the Word of God and to fully appreciate it. But we will find the sword to be one of our choicest weapons in defeating Satan.

Chapter Nine:

Prayer Means Victory

And pray in the Spirit on all occasions with all kinds of prayers and requests. With this in mind, be alert and always keep on praying for all the saints.
Pray also for me, that whenever I open my mouth, words may be given me so that I will fearlessly make known the mystery of the gospel, for which I am an ambassador in chains. Pray that I may declare it fearlessly, as I should.

(Eph. 6:18–20)

It's not enough for the Christian soldier to know the Enemy and to put on the equipment. Complete knowledge of the Enemy and the best equipment in the world are worthless unless the soldier possesses the energy necessary to face the Enemy and to use the equipment. This is where prayer comes in. Notice that immediately following Paul's description of the armour, he makes an appeal for prayer, including prayer for himself and for others:

> *And pray in the Spirit on all occasions with all kinds of prayers and requests. With this in mind, be alert and always keep on praying for all the Lord's people. Pray also for me, that whenever I speak, words may be given me so that I will fearlessly make known the mystery of the gospel, for which I am an ambassador in chains. Pray that I may declare it fearlessly, as I should (Eph. 6:18–20).*

A well-known Christian hymn-writer, William Cowper, made this powerful statement about prayer in one of his poems:

Restraining prayer, we cease to fight;
Prayer keeps the Christian's armour bright;
And Satan trembles when he sees
The weakest saint upon his knees.

To Put the Armour On

Prayer is the power behind the Christian's armour. When we cease to pray, our energy wanes and we soon cease to fight. Prayer is vital if we are going to experience victory in our battle with Satan.

The role of prayer in this armament is threefold. First, prayer is the means by which we *put the armour on*. In the original Greek manuscript, the words 'pray ... on all occasions' in Ephesians 6:18 actually read: 'By means of praying'. In other words, Paul was saying that the way to put on the belt of truth, the breastplate of righteousness, the helmet of salvation and the other pieces of armour is by praying.

This truth is expressed aptly in a well-known Gospel song 'Stand Up for Jesus'. The third verse of this song tells us:

Stand up, stand up for Jesus,
Stand in His strength alone;
The arm of flesh will fail you –
Ye dare not trust your own.
Put on the gospel armour,
Each piece put on with prayer;
Where duty calls or danger,
Be never wanting there.

We need to avoid two extremes in the Christian life. The first extreme is that of doing nothing. Some people believe that we should leave absolutely every decision and area of our life in God's hands, expecting Him to guide each move we make. Slogans such as 'Let go and let God' express this popular belief. Of course, it is important that we surrender our will to the Lord and do not fight His leading in our life. However, we must also remember that dying to self is not enough. Like Christ, we must also be raised from the dead to walk in newness of life (see Rom. 6:4). While God does the raising, we must do the walking. The Lord has given us a mind and a will, and He expects us to make some decisions for ourselves. God does not wake us up in the morning, feed us breakfast and tell us when to read our Bible. If we always expect the Lord to think and act for us, we soon become a nonentity. And God can't use us when we are in this state.

On the other hand, some Christians go to the opposite extreme. They are the ones who believe we should do everything for ourselves. They say, 'OK, God, You've done your part in saving me. I'll take it from here.' Of course, this kind of thinking also leads to failure. We must strike the proper balance in our life, allowing God to work in us and through us to accomplish His purposes.

How does God reveal His will to us and accomplish His will in us? He does it through prayer. Paul makes this clear in Philippians 2:12–13: 'Therefore, my dear friends, as you have always obeyed – not only in my presence, but now much more in my absence – continue to work out your salvation with fear and trembling, for it is God who works in you to will and to act in order to fulfil his good purpose.' In other words, God works *in* us so we can work *out* His will. How does God work is us? He works through His Word, through suffering, through the ministry of His people and through prayer. God works in and through us, and prayer is an important part of this ministry. We put on the armour by faith, and we exercise this faith by means of prayer.

Each morning, before we do anything else, we should first surrender ourselves to the Lord. We need to practise Romans 12:1–2 daily. Before we put on the armour, we must present our body, mind and will as a sacrifice to Him. Then, by faith, we should prayerfully put on each piece of armour. This is something that each of us must do for ourselves. I can't put on the armour for you, and you can't do it for me. But once we have put on the armour, something wonderful happens. We find that God has equipped and prepared us for battle that day.

To Make the Armour Work

Not only is prayer the means by which we put on the spiritual armour, but it is also the power that *makes the armour work*. Merely putting on the armour doesn't accomplish anything for us if we don't have prayer behind it. Prayer gives the Christian soldier the energy, power and strength he needs to face the warfare.

Our obligation as a soldier for Christ is to stand. Ephesians 6 tells us, 'Put on the full armour of God, so that you can take your stand against the devil's schemes.... Therefore put on the full armour of God, so that when the day of evil comes, you may be able to stand your ground, and after you have done everything, to stand. Stand firm then' (vv. 11, 13–14). Jesus Christ has already won the battle. We have, by faith, claimed our inheritance in Christ. Thus, the purpose of our present fight against Satan is to stand firm against his strategies and attempts to rob us of this inheritance.

In the book of Joshua, God's people claimed their inheritance. They stood strong and remained faithful to the Lord. However, in the book of Judges, the people began to bow down before idols. They followed the godless practises of the other nations around them. What happened? God allowed the other nations to invade the Promised Land, and without the Lord's favour, the Israelites could not stand before their enemies. While the Children of Israel still lived in the land of their inheritance, they did not enjoy their inheritance. Other nations came in and robbed them of their enjoyment.

This is what Satan is seeking to do to the Christian. While he can't take our inheritance in Christ away from us, he can keep us from enjoying it. But when our armour is working through prayer, we are able to stand, and Satan is unable to rob us of our blessings. For example, the belt of truth speaks of integrity – having a mind, heart and will that is not divided. What unites the heart, mind and will? Prayer. Praying to the Father in an attitude of worship, adoration and supplication is a unifying force that pulls our lives together (see Phil. 4:6–7). The same is true for the breastplate of righteousness. We are made righteous when we trust Christ as Saviour. However, Satan is constantly accusing us of losing that righteousness. Claiming our righteousness as we pray helps us remember that we have been justified by faith. This enables us to live a sanctified life.

In addition, prayer gives us the strength to walk after we have put on the shoes of the Gospel of peace. Satan wants to destroy our witness. But when we pray, we receive power from the Holy Spirit that enables us to witness: 'But you will receive power when the Holy Spirit comes on you; and you will be my witnesses' (Acts 1:8). We can take courses on evangelism and read every book we can find on witnessing, but unless the Holy Spirit gives us power, we cannot witness. This power comes through prayer. Likewise, when we pray, our faith grows. And as our shield of faith grows stronger, we are better equipped to put out the fiery darts of doubt thrown by the Wicked One.

The armour begins to work when we pray. That's why prayer is so important in the Christian life. Through prayer, we put the armour on. Through prayer, we make the armour work. One of the great heroes of the Old Testament is Nehemiah. I admire this man. He was able to take a piece of wreckage and build a city out of it. It's interesting to note that in the book of Nehemiah, you find Nehemiah praying on ten different occasions. In leading the people in their work, Nehemiah had a sword in one hand and a trowel in the other. Whenever he faced a problem, he prayed about it. He knew prayer was the power behind his armour and his work.

To Help the Army Win

Every good soldier knows the importance of keeping his equipment in proper working order. His armour and weapons must be ready for battle at a moment's notice. Keeping our armour bright and functioning through prayer is even more important for the Christian soldier, for we are continually at war with Satan and must always be prepared. If we lay down our armour for even a minute, Satan will move in and conquer us.

Prayer serves a third vital function in arming ourselves for battle. It not only enables us to put on the armour and to maintain it, but it also enables us to *help the entire army of Christ win the war.* In Ephesians 6:18 we are instructed to pray for all the saints – not just for ourselves: 'And pray in the Spirit on all occasions with all kinds of prayers and requests. With this in mind, be alert and always keep on praying for all the Lord's people.'

Often we have a tendency to think that we are the only ones fighting this battle with Satan. We are sure that we have the most uncooperative church to pastor, the most difficult Sunday school class to teach, the hardest choir to direct, the most unresponsive mission field to work on or the most exasperating family to raise. We mourn our difficult situation. However, we are not alone in this struggle. Every saint is involved, and we need to uplift and encourage our fellow believers by praying for them daily.

Not only are we instructed to pray for *all* the saints, but our prayer life must also be habitual: 'And pray ... on all occasions with all kinds of prayers and requests. ... be alert and always keep on praying' (v. 18). This means that we should pray all kinds of prayers, including prayers of thanksgiving as well as ones of supplication and request. We must also be persistent in prayer. This involves more than just praying again and again for a request until we receive an answer. Prayer must be an integral and continual part of our lives. We should be communicating with God throughout the day. When we fail to seek the Lord's guidance for even the smallest matter, we will experience defeat. After the Israelites' victory at Jericho, Joshua was so confident that he did not seek God's guidance before the battle with Ai. As a result, Joshua's army was soundly defeated (see Josh. 7). When the Gibeonites came to the camp, Joshua didn't pray concerning the situation, and he was tricked into making a false covenant (see ch. 9).

No battle is so easy that we can win it without prayer. Only the Holy Spirit can give us victory, and the Spirit's power is imparted only through prayer. The Holy Spirit not only empowers us for the battle, but He also enables us to pray in the Lord's will (see Rom. 8:26–27; Jude 20). Our prayers should be sincere and heartfelt. As we pray, it is important that we remain alert, praying with our eyes always on the Enemy, lest he move in and defeat us with one of his deceptive tactics. We must be persistent in prayer – no matter how difficult the battle may be.

Praying for other believers is a blessing, not only for them but for us as well. I have some friends who are in places of leadership. It is my joy to pray for them, for in this way, I am able to share in their ministry. Not everyone can be the Apostle Paul, but every person can pray for those God has called into special places of leadership and ministry. Likewise, every believer is strengthened and encouraged by the knowledge that other Christians are praying for him.

Without prayer our spiritual armour will be of little use to us. We must put on each piece of the armour with prayer and then pray continually in order to keep the armour bright and working properly. Besides praying for ourselves, we should pray daily for the needs of our fellow soldiers. With the power of prayer energising our armour, nothing will be able to stop the Christian army from winning the war.

Chapter Ten:

Feed on the Word

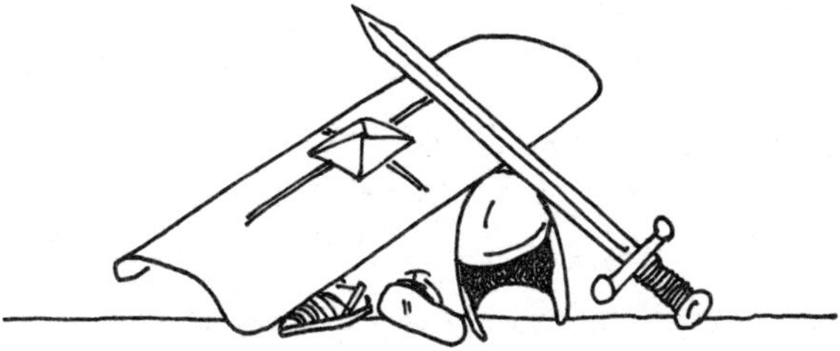

Then Jesus was led by the Spirit into the desert to be tempted by the devil. After fasting forty days and forty nights, he was hungry. The tempter came to him and said, 'If you are the Son of God, tell these stones to become bread.'

Jesus answered, 'It is written: "Man does not live on bread alone, but on every word that comes from the mouth of God.'

(Matt. 4:1–4)

Our best example of how to use the armour properly is the Lord Jesus Christ. Throughout His entire earthly ministry, Christ was assailed by the Wicked One. Satan was constantly watching for an opportunity to defeat Christ. But probably the best known temptation of Christ is recorded in Matthew 4 and Luke 4. It will be helpful to see how Christ handled the temptations Satan put before Him and how He used the armour to defeat Satan.

Matthew 4:1 says, 'Then Jesus was led by the (Holy) Spirit into the wilderness to be tempted (tested) by the devil.' We know Satan by many different names. The name 'Devil' means 'the slanderer'. The name 'Satan' means 'adversary'. We can see by his names that Satan is our enemy. He is our enemy because we belong to Christ, and he is the archenemy of the Lord Jesus Christ. Satan did not want Christ to do the will of God on earth, and he attempted in many ways to stop Him. We shall see three of those ways in this passage.

It's interesting to note the time element of Christ's temptation. Matthew 3 closes with the baptism of our Lord Jesus. The Holy Spirit descended on Him like a dove, and a voice was heard from heaven, saying, 'This is my Son, whom I love; with him I am well pleased' (v. 17). After this marvellous experience, Jesus was led by the Spirit into the wilderness to be tempted by the Devil.

God balances our lives. So often mountaintop experiences lead to valley ones. We need to be especially alert when we've gone through a great spiritual experience, because Satan will be watching for his opportunity. As is often the case in the lives of God's people, a tremendous experience will be followed closely by a low period, a time of testing and trial.

This was true of many of the Old Testament saints. No sooner had Elijah taken care of the false prophets on Mount Carmel than he was so discouraged he wanted to die (see 1 Kings 18–19). There were times in the lives of Jeremiah and Moses when they wanted to quit. Satan knows when we've had an emotional or spiritual experience. He knows we're especially vulnerable then, and he's always standing by to tempt us.

Why Jesus Was Tempted

You may wonder why Christ was tempted by the Devil. It may seem odd that He was *led* by the

Holy Spirit into the wilderness to be tempted by Satan. But God had some very definite purposes for allowing His Son to be tested in this way. I can think of at least three reasons.

To Prepare Him

The first reason why God allowed Christ to be tempted was to prepare Him to be our High Priest. The book of Hebrews tells us,

> *For this reason he had to be made like them, fully human in every way, in order that he might become a merciful and faithful high priest in service to God, and that he might make atonement for the sins of the people. Because he himself suffered when he was tempted, he is able to help those who are being tempted (2:17–18).*

We also read in Hebrews 4:14–16:

> *Therefore, since we have a great high priest who has ascended into heaven, Jesus the Son of God, let us hold firmly to the faith we profess. For we do not have a high priest who*

> *is unable to feel sympathy for our weaknesses, but we have one who has been tempted in every way, just as we are – yet he did not sin. Let us then approach God's throne of grace with confidence, so that we may receive mercy and find grace to help us in our time of need.*

God the Father was preparing God the Son to be our sympathetic, understanding High Priest. Christ knows exactly what we are going through, because He endured the same temptations, frustrations and sufferings while on the earth. Hymn-writer Johnson Oatman, Jr, stated it well when he wrote:

> *Jesus knows all about our struggles,*
> *He will guide till the day is done;*
> *There's not a Friend like the lowly Jesus –*
> *No, not one! No, not one!*

To Expose Satan

The second reason why our Lord was tempted was in order to expose Satan. In reading about the temptation of Jesus, many of us have the mistaken idea that Satan was waiting anxiously to meet the Son of God in a head-to-head confrontation. But this is not Satan's style. The Devil does not want us to know what his tactics are. When we realise that he is tempting us, we are much more capable of resisting him. So he lurks in the darkness and disguises his temptation so we will be deceived into sinning. He knows that if he can keep us in the dark, he will have a much easier time holding us in bondage.

I believe this event in the wilderness dragged Satan out of the darkness into the light, where all of his tactics could be exposed. The key to winning any war is discovering the battle plan of the enemy. God allowed Jesus to be tempted so He could expose Satan's battle plan to us. When we understand the methods Satan used in tempting Jesus, we will better understand how he works and how we can defeat him.

To Teach Us

Jesus was tempted by Satan so He could expose his tactics to us in order to teach us the way to victory. Christ is our example of how to stand firm in the face of temptation.

Many Christians have the mistaken idea

that because Jesus was the sinless Son of God, He was incapable of sinning. Thus, we reason, the temptations posed no real threat to Him. However, the Lord Jesus did not face Satan as God but as a man. He was tempted in every way we are tempted (see Heb. 4:15). He was without sin because He *chose* not to sin. While Jesus could have relied on His divine nature and power, He instead said, 'I'm going to take the same approach in resisting temptation that all of My disciples must take. I want to show them the way to victory.'

Because of Adam's fall into sin, we have inherited a sinful nature. However, Christ became a man in order to show us how to rise above that nature. The temptations Jesus faced and conquered were much more severe than the one Adam succumbed to. For example, Adam was tempted in a beautiful garden, while the Lord Jesus Christ, the second Adam, was tempted in a barren wilderness. The first Adam had every kind of food at his fingertips, yet he deliberately chose to eat the one fruit that God had forbidden. On the other hand, the second Adam had not eaten in 40 days. While the first Adam failed to resist a small temptation, plunging the entire human race into sin and death, the last Adam succeeded in living a sinless life, offering us salvation and eternal life.

Often you and I have a tendency to use our sinful nature as an excuse for giving in to temptation. We say, 'Well, I'm only human. I can't help it if my sinful nature keeps getting the best of me. God knows I can't be perfect. Surely He will be more lenient with me.' But we don't need a new body to defeat Satan. We have the same resources at our disposal that our Lord used when He met Satan in the wilderness. By using these resources and learning from His example, we can resist Satan's temptations just as He did.

How Jesus Was Tempted

The temptations of Jesus reveal to us the areas in which Satan tempts us – physically, emotionally and spiritually. While we tend to think of Christ's first temptation to turn stones into bread as a physical one, Satan used many tactics in that one temptation. The Devil tempts us in these same ways today.

To Satisfy His Needs

One of Satan's most successful strategies is to tempt us to satisfy our needs in a wrong way. In his first attempt at tempting Jesus, Satan employed this effective tactic. Matthew 4:2 tells us, 'After fasting for forty days and forty nights, he was hungry.'

We often tend to forget that the Lord Jesus had a real body. He had the same needs and emotions that we do. He was hungry (see v. 2). He was thirsty (see John 4:7). He grew weary (see Mark 4:38). He wept (see John 11:35). He felt pain (see Isa. 53:5). He died (see Luke 23:46). Christ had just spent 40 days fasting in the wilderness in preparation to meet the Tempter. He was weak from lack of food and rest. Satan took advantage of the Lord's weakened physical condition to attack His natural appetites. The Devil told Him, 'If you are the Son of God, tell these stones to become bread' (Matt. 4:3). This temptation was reasonable. 'After all,' Satan reasoned, 'You are hungry. You have the power to turn stones into bread. Wouldn't God expect You to use your power to take care of yourself?'

Satan frequently uses the natural and God-given functions of the body to tempt us. In themselves these physical needs and desires are not wrong. However, if we satisfy them apart from the will of God, then we are sinning. Thus, even eating and sleeping can be wrong if they are not done to the glory of God. We must remember that a *temptation is an opportunity to satisfy a legitimate need in an illegitimate way*.

The Lord Jesus realised that obeying God's will had to come before the satisfaction of His physical needs. He told Satan, 'It is written, "Man shall not live by bread alone, but by every word that proceeds from the mouth of God"' (v. 4, NKJV). Satan frequently tries to get us to take shortcuts in accomplishing the Lord's will. He whispers in our ear, 'The end result is good, right? If you follow my plan, you will be able to please God much faster. So what's wrong with ignoring His will in this matter as long as your heart's right?' When we listen to Satan, we begin to justify our sins. However, no matter how noble our intentions may be, in God's eyes the end never justifies the means.

To Doubt God's Love

In tempting Jesus to ignore God's will and satisfy His needs, Satan was also trying to cause the Lord to doubt God's love for Him. Satan asked Jesus, in effect, 'Didn't God just tell you, "This is my Son, whom I love; with him I am well pleased"? If the Father loves you so much, why are you hungry? Why hasn't He met your needs?'

One of Satan's most effective deceptions today is the idea that once you become a Christian, you will be free from sorrow, pain and suffering for the rest of your life, as well as for eternity. I hear this kind of Gospel being preached in many places today. These people will tell you, 'God loves you. Once you accept Him, He'll see to it that you will never be sick again. You will never be injured or in pain. Because God loves you, He wants you to have economic success. He wants you to have the biggest car in the neighbourhood and the best job at the factory.' Then when you do experience trials, you are unprepared to handle them. Satan tempts you to doubt God's love, saying, 'If God really loved you, He wouldn't allow this to happen to you. He would take care of you and give you what you want.' If you listen to Satan, you begin to doubt God's love and care. This, in turn, leads to anger and bitterness towards the Lord.

However, we need to remember that God has not promised us an easy life on earth. We will experience persecution and suffering. But this does not mean that the Lord isn't concerned. Many times He allows our pain and suffering *because He loves us* and wants to help us grow stronger.

To Use His Power Wrongly

A third way Satan tempted Jesus was to lure Him to use His power for His own gain. Satan was telling the Lord, 'You have the power and authority to perform this miracle. You will be using your power to help many other people. Why don't You use some of it for Your own needs?'

The temptation to achieve prestige and power and to use this authority for personal gain is very strong today. We face this temptation continually. Society tells us to look out for ourselves and tempts us to believe that power produces happiness. We fall for Satan's temptation to usurp God's authority and use our power to accomplish our will rather than the Lord's. The way a person uses his authority is an indication of whose will he is trying to accomplish.

Jesus refused to use His power for His own gratification. He told Satan, 'It is written' (Matt. 4:4). The Lord was living by the Word of God, for He quoted Deuteronomy 8:3 here. He knew that God did not want Him to use His power to satisfy His needs in the way Satan wanted Him to.

To Separate the Spiritual from the Physical

In answering Satan the Lord Jesus quoted Deuteronomy 8:3: 'He humbled you, causing you to hunger and then feeding you with manna, which neither you nor your ancestors had known, to teach you that man does not live on bread alone but on every word that comes from the mouth of the LORD.' God was not saying in this verse that we do not live by bread but that we do not live by bread *alone*.

Christ knew that Satan was tempting Him to divide His life into separate compartments. He was saying, 'You can't be spiritual all the time. You have to think of Your physical needs.' We face this same temptation today. People often want to separate their soul from their body, the spiritual from the physical.

But as Christ wisely knew, it is impossible to separate the physical from the spiritual. Our body, soul and spirit work together to make us the person we are, and what affects one part also affects the whole. The way in which you use your body affects your spiritual life. Your emotions affect you physically. What you allow your mind to dwell on will have an effect on your emotions. You cannot dissect your life into neat little sections. When you try to separate the physical from the spiritual, it eventually leads to sin.

Jesus told Satan, 'Man shall not live by bread alone, but by every word that proceeds from the mouth of God' (Matt. 4:4, NKJV). The Word of God must control every area of our life – the physical as well as the spiritual. Satan was tempting Christ to ignore God's Word, because he understands how vital it is.

All of life is controlled by the Word of God. God's Word is what gave Joshua victory: 'This Book of the Law shall not depart from your mouth, but you shall meditate in it day and night, that you may observe to do according to all that is written in it. For then you will make your way prosperous, and then you will have good success' (Josh. 1:8, NKJV). We learn several truths about God's Word from these verses. First, God's Word 'proceeds from the mouth of God' (Matt. 4:4, NKJV), into the mouths of His people (see Josh. 1:8). He feeds us His Word. Second, God's Word is able to give us victory and satisfaction. Third, we need *every word* that proceeds out of the mouth of God – not just Psalm 23 or Romans 8.

The Devil was saying to Christ, 'God's holding out on You. I can give You what God will not give You.' But our Lord replied, 'All I need will be given to Me through the Word of God.' When we read and study God's Word, meditate on it and obey it, God will take care of our needs. He has promised to give us what we need when we put Him first in our lives (see Matt. 6:33). Satan would love for us to separate our lives into little pigeonholes. He would love for us to ignore God's Word. When we do, we are easy prey for him. But Jesus, by His example, is saying to us, 'Take up the sword of the Spirit. Don't allow Satan to defeat you with half-truths.

Know your sword well so that you can use it against Satan. Make sure every piece of armour is in place so that he cannot find a vulnerable spot to defeat you.'

Satan tempted Christ to satisfy His needs in a wrong way, to doubt God's love for Him, to use His power illegitimately and to separate His life into compartments. But Jesus did not fall for Satan's temptations. Instead, He used the sword of the Spirit to defeat him. Christ exposed Satan for what he is. Christ's temptations not only prepared Him to be our High Priest, but they also teach us how to defeat the Devil. Victory is possible. Christ has shown us the way. We need to employ the resources He has made available to us, and then we will have 'good success' (Josh. 1:8, NKJV).

Chapter Eleven:

Balance Scripture with Scripture

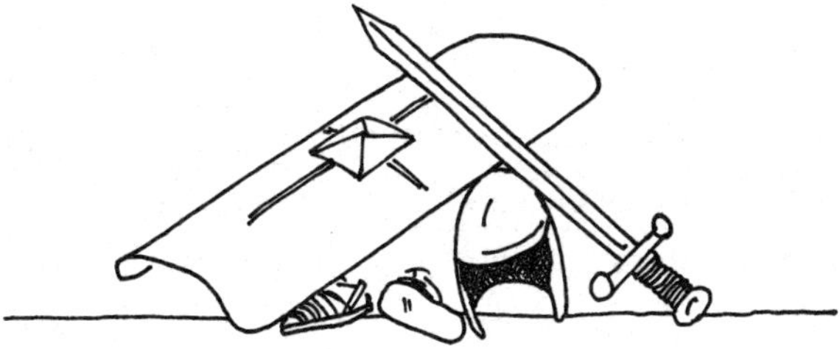

Then the devil took him to the holy city and had him stand on the highest point of the temple. 'If you are the Son of God,' he said, 'throw yourself down. For it is written:

'"He will command his angels concerning you, and they will lift you up in their hands,so that you will not strike your foot against a stone."'

Jesus answered him, 'It is also written: "Do not put the Lord your God to the test."'

(Matt. 4:5–7)

We live in a world filled with sin and temptation. I don't know of any place on the face of the earth where we can go to be free from temptation. Many years ago a religious school stated in its catalogue, 'Our campus is located 15 miles from any known sin.' It is apparent that the administrators of this school did not have a proper understanding of Satan's methods of temptation or of the condition of the human heart. While external circumstances often contribute to our sinning, temptation begins in the heart. Our minds and hearts choose to sin long before we commit the act. And we carry our sinful hearts with us everywhere. Satan and his host of demonic soldiers are always there to tempt us. Even when we are not facing a conscious temptation, Satan can still plant sinful thoughts and attitudes in our minds. In addition, we can never totally isolate ourselves from the world. We will always have to deal with these forces.

We are continuously facing an external enemy (the world), an internal enemy (the flesh) and the infernal Enemy (the Devil). We can't escape them. Jesus couldn't escape temptation either – even when He was standing on the pinnacle of the temple. Matthew 4:5–7 tells us,

> *Then the devil took him to the holy city and set him on the highest point of the temple. 'If you are the Son of God,' he said, 'throw yourself down. For it is written: "He will command his angels concerning you, and they will lift you up in their hands, so that you will not strike your foot against a stone."' Jesus answered him, 'It is also written: "Do not put the Lord your God to the test."'*

Don't Misinterpret the Word

What was the purpose of Satan's second temptation? It is interesting to note the Enemy's strategy in this passage. He took Jesus from the wilderness to the pinnacle of the temple, one of the highest spots on the temple. It was probably 500 feet above the Kidron Valley below. Then Satan tried to convince the Lord to jump, quoting an Old Testament passage as support that He would not be hurt.

Why did Satan use this particular temptation? Several possible reasons have been offered by commentators. Some have asserted that Satan was challenging Christ to prove to the people that He was the Son of God. If Jesus had jumped off the temple and landed safely in front of the huge crowds milling around below, they likely would have believed in Him. Thus, Satan was tempting Jesus to take a shortcut in His ministry.

While this is a viable explanation, I'm not sure that this was Satan's real intent. I think Satan was saying to the Lord Jesus, 'OK, Jesus, You silenced me the first time with the Word of God. But two can play this game. I know what the Bible says. If You insist on answering me from God's Word, then I'm going to use the Word to tempt You.' In this second temptation, Satan was tempting Jesus to test the truth of God's Word. The Devil quoted from Psalm 91:11–12, challenging Jesus to prove that God would really do as He said: 'For he will command his angels concerning you to guard you in all your ways; they will lift you up in their hands, so that you will not strike your foot against a stone.'

Psalm 91 describes the security and safety of those who dwell under the shadow of the Almighty. In this passage, the psalmist was using the imagery of the cherubim in the Holy of Holies to describe God's care for those who abide in Him. Just as the wings of the golden cherubim overshadowed the ark of the covenant, 'He will cover you with his feathers, and under his wings you will find refuge' (v. 4). Later the psalmist added that the Lord has assigned His angels to watch over us, to care for us and to protect us when we fall (see vv. 11–12).

If you compare Satan's quote in Matthew 4:6 with Psalm 91:11, you will discover that he purposely left out a phrase. Psalm 91:11 reads: 'For he will command his angels concerning you to guard you in all your ways'. The child of God has the protection of God in the will of God. But if what we are doing is out of the will of God, the Lord is not obligated to protect us. God, in His grace, will forgive our sins, but God, in His government, has to allow us to suffer the consequences of what we have done. We reap what we sow (see Gal. 6:7). Some Christians have the idea that they can deliberately disobey the Lord and do what they want to do. And then, when they are in trouble, they can run to God and He will rescue them. But they are misinterpreting the Word of God.

Satan knows the Bible better than we do. He frequently uses God's Word as a means of tempting us. He twists certain passages and omits others in an effort to lead us to misinterpret the Word. Misinterpretation of God's Word has not only caused many to sin but has also caused division in the Church. Like Jesus, we must continually seek the Lord's will in the Word, asking for wisdom in 'rightly dividing the word of truth' (2 Tim. 2:15, NKJV).

Don't Isolate a Text

Misinterpreting certain passages is just one of many sins against God's Word that Satan wants us to commit. Another is the temptation to isolate one text from the rest of the Scriptures. One of the greatest problems among believers today is this practise of using passages out of their context to support a particular view.

Satan is a master of division. He knows that if he can divide people's lives, he can conquer them. Likewise, he knows that the easiest way to destroy the Church is by dividing the Word of God. Thus, he is constantly tempting us to divide the spiritual from the physical. He deceives us into believing that what we do with our body has no effect on our soul and spirit.

In tempting Jesus to turn stones into bread, Satan wanted Him to separate the physical from the spiritual. But Jesus knew that the physical must be controlled by the spiritual. Listening to – and feeding on – every word of God was more important to Him than satisfying His physical hunger. He knew that when we are obeying God's will, our physical needs will be taken care of. In teaching the people a short time later, Jesus stated, 'But seek first his kingdom and his righteousness, and all these things will be given to you as well' (Matt. 6:33). When we are seeking God's rule and righteousness, His resources will also be made available to us. However, we can't have God's resources if we are not willing to submit to His rule and obey His righteousness. They must go together.

In this second temptation, Satan was now trying to make Jesus separate the Word of

God from the Word of God. Satan wanted the Lord to claim this one promise literally without balancing it against the rest of God's teachings in His Word. But Jesus told the Devil, 'It is written again, "You shall not tempt the LORD your God"' (Matt. 4:7, NKJV). Christ was quoting Deuteronomy 6:16. The Lord compared the passage Satan quoted with what the verse in Deuteronomy said. He knew that following the first would be disobeying the second.

I believe Dr G. Campbell Morgan was one of the greatest expositors who ever lived. In his book *The Crises of the Christ*, he made a profound statement regarding Christ's words to Satan: 'What infinite value there is in that word "again." How excellent a thing it would be if the whole Church of Christ had learned that no law of life may be based upon an isolated text. It is ever necessary to discover the varied sides of truth, for these limit each other in operation, and create the impregnable stronghold of safety for the soul of man.

'In a study of the heresies of the Church – not a very profitable one, be it said – it will be seen that all these have been based upon Scripture used as the devil uses it – Scripture taken out of its context and out of its relation to the whole of the revelation. Every false teacher who has divided the Church has had an "it is written" on which to hang his doctrine. If only against the isolated passage there had been the recognition of the fact that "again it is written", how much the Church would have been saved.'

We must balance Scripture with Scripture. Notice what Jesus said in Matthew 4:4, NKJV: 'Man shall not live by bread alone, but by every word that proceeds from the mouth of God.' We must live by *every word* given by God in His Word – not just the ones we like. While I know that each of us has favourite books and passages in the Bible, it is vital that we study *all* of God's Word, weighing one passage against another. We must live according to *all* of the Bible's teachings and must guard against turning to the same passage again and again in seeking the Lord's will. 'All Scripture is God-breathed and is useful for teaching, rebuking, correcting and training in righteousness' (2 Tim. 3:16). This does not mean that God can't speak to us through isolated verses. We must simply be careful to interpret any verse in the light of what the rest of Scripture says.

Don't Tempt God

When you are in the will of God, then you can depend on God's care. The Lord will work out His perfect will in your life. Of course, it is not always God's will to deliver us physically from danger. Missionaries are martyred. Christian workers die in automobile accidents. People become ill, and they sometimes die. However, God will never allow anything to harm us spiritually. It may hurt us physically, but it won't harm us. He will work out His perfect plan.

Satan wanted Jesus to test God's protection. But Christ told him, 'It is written again, "You shall not tempt the LORD your God"' (Matt. 4:7, NKJV). He was quoting from Deuteronomy 6:16, NKJV, which reads: 'You shall not tempt the LORD your God as you tempted Him in Massah.' What does it mean to tempt God (to put Him to the test)? It means to put yourself in a situation where God must perform a miracle to rescue you. This can happen in

Christian ministries and churches. However, there is a difference between living by faith and living by chance.

Some years ago, a friend of mine was 'led of God' to quit his job and start his own business. He was sure the Lord was going to bless him. But within a short time, he was begging his boss to take him back again. He lost his resources and his testimony. He had bragged to everyone that God was going to take care of him and his business. However, the Lord didn't bless his business. Why? Because he was out of the will of God. He had not been walking by faith. He was walking by chance. This is why it is so important to know *all* of the will of God. We must balance God's law with God's grace. We must balance His precepts with His promises. As we read the Word of God, we must get to know the mind and heart of God.

The Bible is not a magic book with formulas for success. The Bible is the revelation of the mind of God. Learn this Book. The Bible is the revelation of the heart of God. Love this Book. The Bible is the revelation of the will of God. Live this Book. And don't divorce one from the other.

Constantly as I study the Word of God and prepare messages, I look back at messages I gave five, ten, 15 or 20 years ago. I throw up my hands and say, 'How did I ever preach that?' I had only a segment of the truth. I was not balancing Scripture with Scripture.

In his second temptation Satan was trying to get the Lord Jesus to live by chance and not by faith. He was trying to encourage the Lord to separate the Word of God from the Word of God. Inside each of us is that desire to take chances and to make a public display of our faith. Some Christians are continually running to people and saying, 'Oh, please pray for me. Please help me! I've lost everything!' When the child of God is in the will of God, he will always have the protection and provision of God. But if we stop walking by faith and start walking by chance, God is not obligated to protect us or to provide for us.

This is what happened at Massah when the Israelites tested God. The Lord had just sent them manna from heaven for their hunger. Then the people became thirsty and could find no water. They told Moses, 'Give us water to drink' (Ex. 17:2). The Lord gave them water from a rock but reprimanded the people for tempting Him rather than trusting Him to provide (see v. 7). We tempt God when we dare Him to do something. We test the Lord when we force Him to do a miracle to rescue us because we are out of His will.

Satan frequently uses the Word of God to tempt us. He wants us to sin by misinterpreting the Word, by isolating a text and making it our rule of faith, and by putting God to the test. But we can resist these temptations by learning how to use the sword of the Spirit. We need to read all of the Bible, from Genesis to Revelation. We must study it, meditate on it and penetrate beneath the surface to discover its truths. Allow the Word of God to bring you into the mind of God, the heart of God and the will of God so that you will be able to walk in His will. Then instead of tempting Him, you will be enjoying His will, and Satan's temptations will not cause you to commit some foolish sin.

Chapter Twelve:

Avoid Shortcuts

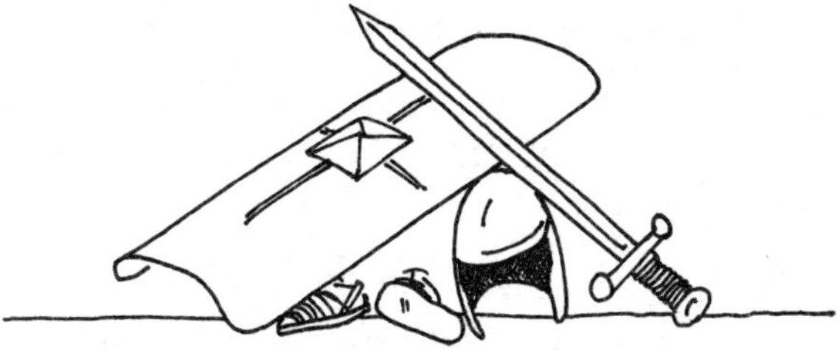

Again, the devil took him to a very high mountain and showed him all the kingdoms of the world and their splendor. 'All this I will give you,' he said, 'if you will bow down and worship me.'

Jesus said to him, 'Away from me, Satan! For it is written: "Worship the Lord your God, and serve him only."'

Then the devil left him, and angels came and attended him.

(Matt. 4:8–11)

It comes as a surprise to some of God's people that Satan is interested in worship. But the issue of worship is what caused Lucifer (Satan) to fall. He wanted to be higher than God and to be worshipped and served like God (see Isa. 14:12–14). He said, 'I will make myself like the Most High' (v. 14). Satan has always wanted man to worship and serve the creature more than the Creator (see Rom. 1:25). And for the most part, he has succeeded.

Most of the people in the world today are not worshipping God; they are worshipping themselves and material possessions. They have exchanged the glory of God for the shame of idolatrous practises (see vv. 21–32). We see this happening even among people who claim to be sophisticated, intelligent and educated. They are not really worshipping God but Satan, for we cannot worship both. We cannot be neutral in our worship. Every person on the face of the earth is worshipping something. If he's not worshipping the true and living God, then in one form or another, he is worshipping Satan.

Even Jesus was faced with the choice of worshipping God or Satan. In his third temptation, the Devil tried to convince Christ to bow down before him. We read in Matthew 4:8–9: 'Again, the devil took him to a very high mountain and showed him all the kingdoms of the world and their splendour. "All this I will give you," he said, "if you will bow down and worship me."' But Jesus did not allow the promise of power and wealth to deter Him from what He knew was right. He told the Devil, 'Away from me, Satan! For it is written: "Worship the Lord your God, and serve him only"' (v. 10).

In the first temptation, Satan asked Jesus to turn stones into bread. It was a temptation to use His power and authority to satisfy Himself. Satan tempted the Lord to *separate the physical from the spiritual.* But Jesus told him, 'Physical bread is not enough, we must also feed on the Word of God' (see v. 4). In the second temptation, the Devil tried to get Jesus to *separate the Word of God from the Word of God.* But Jesus replied, 'We should not put God to the test, we must balance Scripture with Scripture to determine God's will for us' (see v. 7). In this third temptation, Satan was trying to convince the Lord to *separate worship from service*. Christ answered him, 'We cannot serve you and still be worshipping God' (see v. 10).

Satan continually tries to undermine God's Word, for he knows that if he can cause us to doubt its teachings, he can tempt us to sin. Thus, the Devil places questions about God's Word in our minds. He used this tactic when he tempted Christ. In the first temptation, Satan questioned *God's love*. He said, in effect, 'If God really loves You, why are You hungry?' (see v. 3). In the second temptation, the Devil questioned *God's faithfulness*, saying, 'If God the Father loves You and if He is Your Father, then You can trust Him. Throw Yourself off the pinnacle of the temple. See if God is faithful' (see v. 6). In this third temptation, Satan is focusing primarily on *God's hope* for the future.

Joy without Pain

In the Old Testament prophecies concerning the Messiah, it was foretold that He would be ruler over all the kingdoms of the world. In Psalm 2 we read: '"I have installed my king on Zion, my holy mountain." I will proclaim the LORD's decree: He said to me, "You are my son; today I have become your father. Ask me, and I will make the nations your inheritance, the ends of the earth your possession"' (vv. 6–8). Jesus knew that He had received this promise, but He was also acutely aware of the purpose of His coming. He knew that He had not come to reign over the nations at this time. To have accepted Satan's offer would have been going against God's will, but Satan tempted Him by saying, 'You have this future promise. There's glory ahead for You. If You fall down and worship me, I will give it to You now and then You won't have to go to the cross.' The first shortcut Satan tried to cause the Lord to take was that of joy without pain.

A temptation usually is a shortcut, isn't it? Satan will say to us, 'I can give the same thing God offers you, but I'll give it to you in an easier way.' We need to see and learn a principle from this: *Satan's glory always leads to suffering, while God's suffering always leads to glory*. Satan will offer you an easy route to glory. It will look wonderful. All you have to do is obey him, worship him. But eventually that glory will turn into shame and suffering. On the other hand, the Lord Jesus offers you suffering: 'take up the cross, and follow Me' (Mark 10:21, NKJV; see also 8:34). But the suffering He asks you to endure will perfect you and will ultimately lead to glory (see 2 Cor. 4:17).

Satan offers you great joy and pleasure, which leads to pain. But the Lord Jesus offers you suffering and death to self, which leads to joy and pleasure. 'You will fill me with joy in your presence, with eternal pleasures at your right hand' (Ps. 16:11). This idea seems contradictory, but that is exactly why Satan can deceive so many. According to human reasoning, joy and pleasure should lead to glory. We find it hard to believe that suffering and death could lead to glory. God's ways are incomprehensible if you use human reasoning alone.

First, Satan tempted Christ to live for the physical, not for the spiritual. Then he tempted Him to live by chance, not by faith. Now he is tempting Him to live for the temporary, not the permanent. Satan tempts us in these same ways, and he is often successful. Many people are sacrificing the eternal on the altar of the temporal. Satan tempts them with some glorious, new idea of how to quickly attain happiness and success. They believe his lie and end up worshipping Satan. And when you worship Satan, you end up serving him.

Worship without Service

Satan tempted Christ to worship him, for he knew that if Christ would do so, he would soon be serving him. This is why our Lord quoted from Deuteronomy 6:13: 'Fear the LORD your God, serve him only and take your oaths in his name.' Did you notice that Satan had not said one word about service? '"All this I will give you," he said, "if you will bow down and worship me"' (Matt. 4:9). The tense of the Greek verb for 'you will worship' indicates an action that would occur just once. How many times have you heard that lie of Satan? 'Just do it once. You don't have to do it again. Besides, everyone is doing it.' Satan said, 'Just fall down once and worship me.' But the Lord Jesus replied 'Worship the Lord your God, and serve him only' (v. 10).

Christ was introducing an entirely new element here – that of service. Whatever you worship, you serve. If you worship yourself, your pleasures, your comfort, your fame and your ambitions, you will serve yourself. Everything you do will have a selfish motive behind it. If you worship pleasure and the enjoyments of this world, you will serve the world. You will begin to see things from the world's perspective, and the world will have your time and attention. Whatever you worship becomes your master. That is why God wants our worship.

To worship God means to bring Him our adoring obedience and praise. He is worthy of all praise (see Rev. 4:11). He alone is worthy of all worship. So why should we worship Satan? What could possibly make us want to worship him? Or course, he comes disguised as 'an angel of light' (2 Cor. 11:14). But when you worship Satan, you are believing lies, because Satan is a liar (see John 8:44). When you worship Satan, you are destroying and not building up, because Satan is a lion (see 1 Pet. 5:8), and a destroyer (see Ps. 17:4, NKJV). When you worship Satan you are out of the will of God. You are walking in darkness, because Satan is the prince of darkness (see Eph. 6:12). There are many people who, even in their religious exercises, are actually worshipping Satan. All idolatry is satanic. Paul made it very clear in 1 Corinthians 10:18–21 that when a person bows down to an idol, he is actually bowing down to demonic forces. We don't bow down to grotesque, ugly idols of wood and stone or silver and gold. No, we bow down to the idols of money, power, prestige, fame, social acceptance and success. These are the gods we worship today.

Not only do we serve what we worship, but we also begin to make sacrifices for what we serve. Therefore, every person should pause and take inventory of his life, asking himself, *for what or whom am I sacrificing*? For example, someone may say that he just doesn't have the time and energy to read his Bible and pray in the morning before he goes to work. Yet the same person can rise at 2.30 a.m. to go fishing. Someone else may say, 'I'm too tired to go to church today. Besides, I have a headache and feel too sick to sit through a service.' But then he reads about a sale or special show taking place that day. Suddenly, he feels well again. We make sacrifices for what is important to us. Jesus warned us against worshipping something or someone other than God, for He knew that worship is followed by service and sacrifice. He stated: 'Do not store up for yourselves treasures on earth … . But store up for yourselves treasures in heaven … . For where your treasure is, there your heart will be also' (Matt. 6:19–21).

We serve and sacrifice for whatever we worship. But even more dangerous than this is the fact that we give *ourselves* to what we worship. Soon we have become like the god we serve. Psalm 115 talks about the futility of idol worship. We read: 'Those who make them will be like them, and so will all who trust in them' (v. 8). Our lives reflect what we worship, and we are controlled by it. That's why we must make sure we are worshipping God alone so that our lives are patterned after His image.

A Crown without a Cross

Satan often tempts us to believe that we can experience joy without also having pain or that we can worship him without serving him. He tempted Jesus with these illusions. However, the Lord made it clear that worship and service cannot be separated. Satan then tried to convince Jesus that He could inherit His crown without having to bear the cross first.

We live in a society that has been deceived by Satan into believing that there are shortcuts to success. The Devil offers us a quick and 'easy' road to what we want. He told Eve, 'All you have to do is eat this fruit, and you can immediately become like God, knowing good and evil' (see Gen. 3:5). In fact, the Lord Jesus faced this temptation several times during His ministry. Peter tried to talk Him out of going to the cross. In Matthew 16 Peter said, 'Never, Lord! ... This shall never happen to you!' (v. 22). In John 6 Jesus had just fed the 5,000. The people were full and satisfied. As a result, they wanted to crown Jesus as king (see v. 15). Once again Christ faced the temptation to take a shortcut to His kingdom and avoid going to the cross. But Jesus knew that God cannot be glorified without a cross and that even He, the Son of God, could not glorify His Father apart from the cross. Therefore, He 'humbled himself by becoming obedient to death – even death on a cross!' (Phil. 2:8).

If Jesus had to endure the cross, why should we believe that we can avoid bearing our cross? In every life there is a Gethsemane. With every Gethsemane comes a Calvary. And under every crown is a cross. Peter learned that lesson. In fact, suffering and glory are linked together throughout his first letter. We cannot receive the glory without having first suffered. Satan says to us, 'I can give you the easy way.' But his 'easy' way turns out to be very hard. Likewise, he tells us, 'Worship me just this once and I will give you glory.' But that glory will always lead to suffering. Once we worship Satan, we begin serving him before we even realise it. Soon we are sacrificing for him. Then we are becoming like him. Then judgment comes.

On the other hand, suffering for the Lord's sake always leads to glory. Instead of living for what is temporary, Christians should concentrate on what has eternal value. For the Christian, the path of service is not easy. We may have many hardships along the way. While Satan's path may appear easier, his road always leads to hell. But when we pick up our cross and follow Jesus in the path of suffering, we know that an eternity of glory awaits us in heaven.

In the temptations of Jesus, we discover the fiery darts that Satan is hurling at us daily. Just as the Devil tempted Jesus to turn stones into bread, he tempts us to question the love of God and to separate the physical from the spiritual. Likewise, Satan tempts us to 'throw ourselves off the temple' – to test God's faithfulness and see if He really keeps His word. The Devil wants us to separate Scripture from Scripture so he can deceive us into worshipping him by separating worship from service. He causes us to worship things or people instead of God. He wants us to believe that his road to success is easy and that we can have joy without pain and suffering.

Often it appears that we are losing our battle against temptation and sin. But Christ has won the war for us. He has given us the same resources that He used in overcoming the Tempter – the indwelling Spirit of God, the inspired Word of God and the interceding Son of God. When Jesus was tempted, He allowed Himself to be guided by the Holy Spirit. He used the Word of

God to combat Satan's arguments. He quoted from the Scriptures and applied them with skill and wisdom. Because He endured every temptation we face, Jesus Christ knows exactly how we feel. He is our sympathetic High Priest and is constantly interceding on our behalf. Put on your spiritual armour and allow Him to give you the victory.

Other books by Warren W. Wiersbe:

Abide

Understanding the secrets of living for Jesus

Do you know the secret of living?

In order to bear fruit, we must abide in Christ . . .

What is the secret of abiding?
It is obeying; give God your will.

What is the secret of obeying?
It is loving; give God your heart.

What is the secret of loving?
It is knowing; give God your mind.

Christ gave His disciples complete instructions for living the abundant life. And He speaks to us today through His Word, saying: 'This life can be yours as well!'

Other books by
Warren W. Wiersbe:

Little Book of Big Words

Key words of the Christian life

Justification. Adoption. Regeneration. Propitiation. Imputation. Redemption. Sanctification. Mediation. Intercession. Formed. Predestination. Glorification.

Only when you understand these big words from the Bible will you be able to live out what they teach. These 'doctrinal words' help you know what a Christian is, what Christ has done for you, and what he wants to do for you.

Wiersbe's little guide is an invaluable resource whether you're a new believer or a seasoned Bible teacher. The accessible definitions found here will guide you through Scripture and throughout the Christian life.

Other books by Warren W. Wiersbe:

On Being a Servant of God

Key words of the Christian life

Sometimes people lose sight of the core of their ministry. They feel overwhelmed by the needs that surround them on a daily basis.

Wise and well-loved pastor Warren Wiersbe invites ministry leaders to listen in on thirty short 'armchair chats' to encourage and strengthen them for service. He shares what he wishes he had known about ministering to others when he began his own Christian pilgrimage.

'Ministry,' he says, 'takes place when divine resources meet human needs through loving channels to the glory of God.' With this new edition of a classic book the next generation of ministry leaders can take advantage of Wiersbe's years of wisdom.

Stand
Putting on the
full armour of God
Warren W. Wiersbe